National Heraldry of the World

Geoffrey Briggs

National Heraldry of the World

illustrated by Glenn Steward,
B. L. Ainsworth and Carol Kane

 J. M. Dent and Sons Limited   London

First published 1973
© Text, Geoffrey Briggs, 1973
© Illustrations, J. M. Dent & Sons Ltd, 1973

Printed in Great Britain by
Lowe & Brydone (Printers) Ltd
Thetford · Norfolk
for
J. M. DENT & SONS LTD
Aldine House · Albemarle Street · London

ISBN: 0 460 07834 8

Preface

Many books have been written in the past on the subject of National Flags, and many more appear each year. Indeed, flags must represent the one branch of heraldry with which everyone is at least acquainted, and there can be few people in the world who are ignorant of their significance. Very few books have been written on the subject of National Heraldry. None has been published in recent years. The amazing popular display of heraldry which appears on the occasion of a British coronation, for instance, is ample illustration of the numerous popular misconceptions which prevail with regard to the subject. There is a very common, but erroneous, idea that since there are national flags which all subjects may display, so must those same subjects equally be entitled to display the so-called 'National Arms'. Nothing could be further from the truth.

The general neglect of the subject of 'National Arms and State Emblems' must certainly be attributable to some cause. In fact there are several such causes. The popular manuals of heraldry, by and large, either omit all mention of it, or gloss over it in almost indecent haste. A far more important factor, however, has been the lamentable insularity of outlook which has been so prevalent in the past. If we are to survive in the modern world we must broaden our horizons. Present-day conditions suggest that it is advisable, if not imperative, for the peoples of the world to understand one another more clearly. National Flags are clearly a matter of almost universal interest. They are often a source of intense national pride and arouse a patriotic spirit in the people. They are of great interest to the peoples of other nations because of their historical associations. National Arms, on the other hand, are of even greater significance because it is through them that the nations proclaim their sovereign status; they virtually embody the spirit of the State since through them the State is presented to the world.

The purpose of this book is to set out clearly in not too technical terms the precise significance of National Arms and to explain their origins and characteristics. Within its pages there will be found a complete collection of the Arms and Emblems of all the truly sovereign and independent states in the world at the time of writing. Considerations of space have made it impossible for us to include also the arms and emblems of constituent states and republics, colonies, and associated and protected states.

We extend our sincere and grateful thanks to all those, at all diplomatic levels, whose generous assistance has made the compilation of this book a possibility. Without them it most certainly could not have been produced. Likewise we thank all those who have assisted in the production of the book from reading it in manuscript and proof onwards. Without them it would inevitably have been inferior.

Finally, we would impress upon all who read this book and consult its pages in the future that it is designed as a work of reference no less than one of general interest. *In most, if not all, countries it is an offence to use or display the Royal or State Arms or Emblem without authority, and every care should be taken not to use or display any part of any of the Arms and Emblems herein illustrated without first ascertaining from the authority concerned whether this is in order and seeking permission from the appropriate competent authority.*

Introduction

It is a saying no less true today than it was some sixteen centuries ago, that 'Things more excellent than any symbol are expressed through symbols'. Long before Man could read or write he employed symbols. Long before the days of heraldry, kings and their peoples employed symbols for identification and for purposes of government and ceremonial. National Arms are but a refinement of this practice.

From time immemorial the human race has made extensive use of emblems and symbols as a means of expression and communication, particularly to convey intangible ideas. This page is an assembly of conventional symbols whereby the author communicates his ideas to the reader. Even today Man uses symbols to express ideas for which words prove inadequate. St Patrick selected the shamrock to illustrate his sermon on the Holy Trinity and mathematicians habitually and constantly employ a veritable host of notational symbols.

Perhaps the most intangible concept of all is that of identity, which involves not only the individual but also his relationships with other individuals. Man is a gregarious, yet somewhat anti-social, being; consequently we find, from the earliest times, emblems and symbols serving as a means of identification both personal and collective. The comparatively modern system of heraldry is a means of identification *par excellence*, yet it is but the medieval adaptation of an extremely ancient and widespread tradition which, divested of the semi-magical aura which had surrounded it in remote antiquity, was made to produce a symbolic code for everyday use.

From the time when Man so far forsook his more obviously animal ways to the extent that he began to live in groups, he has ceased to be a true individual; he has tended to become, more and more, an element in a larger unit. Although this may at first have been little better than an animal herd, Man was no longer entirely self-sufficient; he was one of a group with responsibilities outside himself and so was obliged partially to identify himself with his fellows. Here we have the beginnings of group identity. The tribe (and later the State) and its religion made use of devices of significance to the group as a whole, which served both to characterize it and to distinguish it from others. This means of identification of the tribe or State or, as we now should say, nation is the subject of our present study; National Arms and

Emblems are the direct successors, if not the lineal descendants, of the old tribal emblems.

Pre-heraldic symbols and their influence

The origin of heraldry has long been, and is likely to remain indefinitely, a matter of controversy; yet the indications are that the earliest coats-of-arms are derived from military banners and moulded ensigns, which had long functioned in a quasi-heraldic manner. Indeed, some of them persisted into historical times and have been taken over by true heraldry.

Although heraldry is a phenomenon of Western Christendom, the use of ensigns and banners has been known everywhere and at all times, so that it need cause no surprise to find analogous systems in places which have only relatively recently been exposed to European influence. Indeed, it has been suggested that Europe itself owes heraldry to the Saracens from whom, it is claimed, the Crusaders adopted it. This suggestion has not, however, been generally received.

Whatever the true nature of the ensigns of the Hebrew tribes may have been, we have scriptural authority for their existence. It is not unlikely that they were inspired by those of the Egyptians, among whom not only each battalion but each company also had its own particular ensign. The lion traditionally associated with the Tribe of Judah currently appears in the Imperial Emblem of Ethiopia. The Menorah, the seven-branched candlestick of the Tabernacle and Temple, was proclaimed the official emblem of the State of Israel on 10 February 1949.

Coming to Classical times, we find that the Greeks had no regular standard, but we learn also that a scarlet flag was sometimes used as a signal to join battle on both land and sea. The Persians carried a golden eagle as a royal standard, whilst the Parthians had banners of silk. Yet it is with Roman civilization and the Roman military discipline that we approach most nearly our present-day ideas. To the Romans we owe a great deal, not least in the field of government and law. Although the earliest Roman standard is said to have been a bundle of hay held aloft on a spear, in the time of the manipular arrangement of the legion each maniple had its particular badge likewise borne on a staff. The eagle, which originally was the standard of the first maniple, after the time of Marius became that of the whole legion. In the place of the animals, which had formed the badges of the several maniples, was then borne an outstretched hand. The cohorts which replaced the maniples under a later arrangement, after the time of Trajan adopted the *draco*, which they took over from the Parthians. This, as the name implies, took the form of a dragon and consisted of the head and jaws made of silver, the rest of the body being formed of coloured silk, so that when the wind blew down the gaping throat the body was inflated. This *draco* may be seen on various monuments among the standards of foreign nations. It may well have been taken over by our British ancestors and survives today in the Welsh dragon.

The eagle, as the standard of the Roman legion, came to represent the military might of Imperial Rome. It had, however, another significance. It was one of the customary sacred attributes of the Greek god Zeus with whom the Romans identified their god Jupiter. Since he was the chief Roman deity the eagle became the State Emblem of Rome. The Roman army had other standards too. The *vexillum*, for example, was borne by the cavalry. This was a square piece of cloth suspended from the cross-bar of a staff and may have carried the image of the reigning emperor. With the adoption of Christianity as the official religion of the Empire under Constantine, this image was replaced by the Greek *Chi-Rho* monogram of Our Lord. This standard was known as the *Labarum*. In all these standards we have an expression of divinity; the eagle represented Jupiter, the image of the emperor represented his genius, and the monogram represented Christ himself. Obviously the standard represented a tutelary deity and was, in fact, enshrined in the headquarters building of a Roman fortress. The worst disgrace which could befall a legion was the loss of its standards. The same theme is found, too, on military shields; those of the legionaries bore Jupiter's thunderbolt, whilst in the mosaic at Ravenna representing the Imperial Court, Justinian is attended by a warrior carrying a circular green shield upon the surface of which is clearly depicted the golden monogram.

On Christmas Day, 800, Charlemagne was crowned in St Peter's at Rome. Claiming to be the heir of the former Western emperors, he is said to have adopted as his ensign the eagle which he had placed conspicuously on his palace at Aachen. This eagle has had a considerable influence upon the heraldry of future empires. From Charlemagne it passed to the later emperors of the Holy Roman Empire and from them and their chosen successors, the German kings, it passed to those who held office as imperial functionaries and so became firmly established as an imperial symbol. Hence it has often appeared in imperial coats-of-arms. Not only the Holy Roman, Austrian and German empires have made use of it; it has appeared in the arms of those of France and Russia. In the last instance it is more probably a case of inspiration by the Byzantine eagle which, in turn, may have been a re-evocation of the Roman bird. Byzantium certainly was the source of inspiration for the eagles which have appeared in the heraldry of the Balkans. Still the Roman eagle endures, for it has been transmitted via the respective empires to the modern State Arms of the Federal Republics of Austria and Germany. It formerly made its appearance, as might have been expected, as a part of the Royal Arms of Italy.

It is obvious that there is a remarkable degree of continuity in national emblems. In addition to the dragon, which has served for both Wales and Wessex, and also as a Supporter to the Royal Arms in Tudor days, British royal heraldry affords an even more interesting example of continuity; one in which there is, moreover, no trace of a derivative transmission. In the time of Charlemagne, Witikind, in the land between the Weser and the Elbe, used a red banner bearing the figure of a white horse. Now this is the very area from which the Saxon invaders of Britain came and the traditional names of their leaders are Hengist and Horsa, both words signifying a horse. By the twelfth century Henry the Lion held most of this territory, known as Westfalen, and used this self-same banner for the land. At a later date the area was divided; one part passed to the prince-archbishops of Cologne and retained the old name, whilst the remainder, after passing through the hands of the counts of Askania and others, eventually came into the possession of the dukes of Brunswick. Both the archbishops and the dukes used the white horse on red as the arms of the territory; the old banner had attained armorial status. Subsequently the House of Brunswick secured the title of Hanover, and as the House of Hanover succeeded to the British throne. With them came their arms which, in an abbreviated form, took their place among the other components of the Royal Arms. With the operation of the Salic Law, upon the death of William IV in 1837 the Hanoverian representation was no longer vested in the British Crown and the arms were accordingly omitted. The kingdom of Hanover ultimately came to form part of that of Prussia and so became part of Germany. The particular territory which we have been considering presently forms part of the German *Land* of Nordrhein-Westfalen, the arms of which duly incorporate the white horse. This example is of considerable interest, not only because it affords an example of a pre-heraldic banner giving rise to a historical coat-of-arms, but also because it illustrates the totemic element which has all too often been overlooked in heraldic studies.

The examples so far given truly belong to ethnic groups because they date from such remote times and, in their origins, antedate heraldry by several centuries. A far greater number of National Arms, however, display a totally different origin, since the above are exceptional, and have a different significance. Before we proceed to examine these more closely, it will be of considerable assistance if we get our subject in perspective. This we shall do by considering the essential nature of National Arms.

National Arms

National Arms, or Arms of Sovereignty and Dominion as they should more strictly be called, differ from other armorial bearings in many respects, and their precise significance should be kept carefully in mind. They stand, not for any particular area of land, but for the intangible sovereignty vested in the rulers thereof. They properly belong to kingdoms and states and are annexed, as it were, to these but are borne by their representative rulers or heads of state. They are ensigns of public authority, strictly speaking, and are not necessarily, nor are they in fact, hereditary. They pass by conquest. If a subject should ascend a throne, he would customarily lay aside those arms which had hitherto been his by personal right and thenceforth use only those of the dominion to which he had succeeded. Nevertheless, he would be under no obligation to do so; he might, if he so chose, adopt entirely different and distinct arms. A dynastic change which introduces new sovereignties may introduce new elements into the arms; on the other hand this may prove to be impracticable. A ruler ascending a throne by election may choose to show this by combining his family arms in some way with those of the State; in this case the usual method has been by placing the family arms, in an escutcheon, upon those of the State. By way of summary we may say that National Arms are continuing, but not necessarily immutable. A change of regime may totally extinguish them. The one thing which is absolutely certain is that their display is not to be accorded to subjects. They are the symbolic representation of the sovereignty of the State and any use to which they may be put must be fully compatible with this.

National Arms are as varied as the States to which they appertain. They fall into two main categories; one is clearly heraldic, the other is not. Yet this is largely an artificial arrangement, though a convenient one, because even the purely pictorial devices serve armorial ends and are frequently *officially* designated 'Arms' despite their not being centred upon a shield. The presence or absence of a shield is largely an accidental consequence of the history of the State. For example, Europe has always been within the heraldic sphere whilst Africa and Asia have come under heraldic influence only as a result of contacts with Europe. Outside Europe we must regard heraldry as derivative, but even there heraldry has on occasion been abandoned. This has been due to its regal associations.

Historical considerations are of the utmost importance. Having said that, we can proceed to examine our subject in greater detail. Dealing first of all with those States which make use of devices which are obviously heraldic in character, we shall begin with the older European monarchies, since these may be said to have established the practice. Two in particular, the United Kingdom and Sweden, merit our special attention because their Royal Arms, when studied in the light of their historical development, are of great value for the illustration of many aspects of the subject.

The earliest coat-of-arms so far discovered is that of Geoffroy V (Plantagenet), Count of Anjou, who became the father of King Henry II of England. The chronicler Jean Rapicault relates the story of the count's marriage to the Princess Mathilda of England in 1127 and informs us that when his royal father-in-law, King Henry I, bestowed the accolade upon him he hung about his neck a shield bearing golden lions. This very shield is clearly depicted on the enamelled plate which was suspended above his tomb in Le Mans Cathedral in 1151. The *Chronique d'Ernoul* refers to the arms of the King of England in 1157, but unfortunately does not describe them; nor does a shield of arms appear upon the seal of Henry II. In 1189, however, the first Great Seal of Richard I, his son and successor, shows his mounted figure carrying a shield displaying a single lion rampant facing the sinister. Lions are particularly common among the arms of the descendants of these early

Plantagenets, and it is hard not to conclude that a lion coat of some kind was used by King Henry II and probably by his grandfather Henry before him.

Lions could easily have been regarded as a royal emblem in the same way that the eagle represented the royal dignity. The Norwegian lion was adopted about the end of the twelfth or early in the thirteenth century, the present form of the arms coming into use about 1285. The lions of Denmark came into use in the twelfth century and their precise aspect was for long unsettled. Sweden will be considered in more detail shortly. In 1198 the second Great Seal of Richard I of England displays the three lions *passant guardant* (the so-called 'leopards' of England) which have remained the arms of that kingdom ever since. This lion coat remained in use alone until 1340, when Edward III claimed the throne of France by right of his mother. He thereupon, in emphasis of his claim, quartered the Arms of France with those of his own kingdom; and thereby instituted an innovation which was to endure for some centuries. His successor, Richard II, who placed himself under the patronage of St Edward the Confessor, retained exactly the same arms yet impaled this combined coat with that posthumously attributed to his patron. This practice died with him. The succession of the Lancastrian, Yorkist and Tudor sovereigns produced no more radical change in the arms than a reduction in the number of the fleurs-de-lys to three; even this was done only to bring the arms which they bore for France into line with the coat as then borne in that kingdom. In addition to the shield the Royal Arms, of course, include crest and supporters. These also developed and became settled in their present form at the beginning of the next century.

From the seventeenth century onwards we find a more rapid sequence of changes. In 1603 Queen Elizabeth I died and the new sovereign was James VI of Scotland who succeeded as James I. He added to the Royal Arms quarterings for Scotland and Ireland. The shield then bore four quarters; in the first and fourth appeared the arms of his predecessor, in the second Scotland, and in the third Ireland. The crest remained the English lion set upon the crown, whilst the dragon supporter was replaced by the unicorn of Scotland. This arrangement was continued by Charles I, who fell upon the scaffold in 1649. England then, for the only time in its history, became (nominally) a republic.

This was an unprecedented event and had heraldic, no less than political, consequences. The former royal display was at first completely abandoned and on THE GREAT SEALE OF ENGLAND IN THE FIRST YEAR OF FREEDOM BY GOD'S BLESSING RESTORED two cartouches appear: one bearing the cross of St George for England, the other the harp for Ireland. In 1655 a new Great Seal came into use and bore on its obverse a complete achievement. This is of great interest because it was obviously based upon the former royal arms while at the same time showing a nice understanding of their connection with the person of the monarch. Once again, the shield was divided into four quarters. In this instance the first and fourth bore St George's cross, the second the saltire of St Andrew and, in the third quarter, the harp retained its accustomed place. At that time there was no St Patrick's cross, which really has nothing to do with that saint. The royal helmet, mantling and crest were reintroduced as was also the crowned lion supporter, the unicorn being replaced by the former dragon. The motto, instead of the royal *Dieu et mon droit*, became *Pax quaeritur bello*.

Upon the restoration of the monarchy, Charles II continued to use the arms, etc., borne by his father. So did his brother, James II, who was succeeded upon the throne by his elder daughter and son-in-law as the joint monarchs William III and Mary II. This is remarkable in that during the reign of the earlier Mary England had actually had a king consort; with the second Mary we find joint monarchs, although the actual royal power lay in William's hands. We are repeatedly, and consistently, told by all the manuals that, during the lifetime of Mary, the Royal Arms were borne impaled. There is absolutely no official record of any such arrangement. There was a single coat which consisted of the arms borne by James II but upon which was placed a smaller escutcheon of the arms of William's paternal House of Nassau. It is usually asserted that this was done in token of his being an *elected* monarch; in fact he merely followed normal continental European practice.

On the death of William III, Queen Anne bore the arms of her father James II; yet within a very few years a constitutional change made a change in the Royal Arms expedient. This change was the Union with Scotland, 6 March 1707, which was indicated by remarshalling the contents of the shield. These then continued to display four quarters, but the first and fourth now bore the *impaled* Arms of England and Scotland, France was relegated to the second quarter, whilst the third quarter remained as before. Indeed, it has never changed since it was first introduced in 1603.

In 1714 the House of Hanover, in the person of George I, succeeded to the throne. He did not follow continental practice but introduced an abbreviated version of his arms as Elector of Hanover into the fourth quarter. This quarter contained not only the arms of Brunswick, Lüneburg and Hanover, but also an inescutcheon to represent the office of Arch-Treasurer of the Holy Roman Empire. On the Union with Ireland, 1 January 1801, the opportunity was taken to omit the arms of France, which had for so long represented an empty claim which was, moreover, no longer even remotely conceivable because the revolution had extinguished the monarchy in that country. The arms were once more remarshalled to show England in the first quarter, Scotland in the second, Ireland in the third, with England once again in the fourth. Over all was placed an inescutcheon containing what had previously been in the fourth quarter and this shield was ensigned by the Electoral bonnet. When Hanover became a kingdom this bonnet was replaced by the Royal Crown.

When William IV died in 1837, Victoria could not succeed to the throne of Hanover, where the Salic Law operated, and so the final reorganization of the shield took place. The Arms of Hanover were omitted and the Royal Achievement became as it is today. It will be seen that the development of the Royal Arms of the United Kingdom admirably illustrates the way in which National Arms can reflect territorial representation, whether actual or pretended, in addition to showing the effects of changes in both dynasty and regime. The Royal Arms of Sweden illustrate the subject in perhaps an even better way. That country has had more changes in dynasty than most and the stages are clearly indicated in its arms.

The seal of King Erik Knutsson (1208–16) presents heraldic decoration in the form of two crowned leopards facing each other, but these are probably not intended as real heraldic charges; no arms are known for him or for his successor John Sverkersson, who was succeeded in 1222 by the six-year-old Erik Eriksson, the son of Erik Knutsson and of Rikissa, daughter of King Waldemar I of Denmark. He bore three crowned leopards in pale, the arms of his mother's family, yet they could not have been exclusively the Danish Royal Arms for, had they been so, he could not have used them. He was succeeded by Knut the Tall who deposed him between 1229 and 1234. Knut was probably a member of the Erik family and it is significant that his arms, which are known from a tapestry, are entirely different; they are obviously family arms used as State Arms.

In 1250 the Folkunga dynasty came upon the scene in the person of Waldemar, the son of Erik's sister. He did not use the arms of his family, but kept to the three leopards used by Erik. On his *secretum* he used two crowns in pale, but they are certainly not armorial charges for they stand freely in the field of the seal; their purpose is to symbolize the king. The other members of this dynasty bore the family arms which Magnus Ladula (1275–90) augmented by crowning the lion, a proof of the importance of the lion as a symbol of royalty. These arms have come to be associated with Gotaland, the southern part of Sweden, yet it is clear from the legend on his seal (SIGILLUM: MAGNI: DEI: GRACIA: REGIS: SWEORUM) that the Folkunga Arms as State Arms represented the whole of Sweden.

The arms so far used, those of Knut the Tall and the Folkunga dynasty, were Swedish in origin and were family arms converted by regal and official use into the Arms of the State. A different situation arose in 1363 when Duke Albrecht I of Mecklenburg, who had married a sister of Magnus Eriksson, attacked his brother-in-law and the next year secured the proclamation of his own son as King of Sweden. What arms was the new king to bear? Here was a nice problem. Although he had some claim to the Folkunga Arms through his mother, Albrecht could hardly with decency adopt the arms of the family he had driven out of the land, even though those very arms had been used as the arms of the State. As a feoffee or as heir of his father he was entitled to bear some combination of the Arms of Mecklenburg, Schwerin and Rostock; but as King of Sweden these would be inappropriate and he

would need some insignia of his own representing his newly acquired territory. He had to create a new coat and very naturally he adopted as the charge in his shield the crown, the symbol of his dignity. Yet by so doing he was not creating an entirely new coat-of-arms as has been supposed; his own arms of Mecklenburg would have made him familiar with the crown as a charge. No doubt Albrecht saw that he could not politically use his ancestral bull's head in Sweden and so naturally retained its crown as a convenient symbol, arranging three of them on the shield. This is a typical medieval arrangement giving convenient symmetry. Such an arrangement duly appeared upon his seal in 1364.

When in 1389 Albrecht was defeated and captured at Falköping by Margaret, Queen of Norway and Denmark, the three Scandinavian countries were united. One of her *secreta* shows a shield charged with three crowns, but this is said to represent the union: in another seal Sweden is represented by the Folkunga Arms. Her successor, Erik of Pomerania, used both the three crowns and the Folkunga Arms to represent Sweden. His second Great Seal has a shield quartered, the quarters separated by a cross with an escutcheon over all. This escutcheon shows the arms of Norway while the four quarters show respectively the three leopards of Denmark, the crowns, the bendlets and lion of the Folkungar, and the griffin of Pomerania. A different arrangement appeared on the ship's flag of this period which was formerly in the Marien Kirche at Lübeck. This displayed the Arms of Denmark, Sweden, Norway and Pomerania in the four quarters of the flag separated by a white cross.

When in 1436 the Swedes renounced their allegiance to King Erik, a new State Seal was required. This represents the national patron saint, St Erik, wearing armour with an open crown on his head; his left hand supports a shield charged with three crowns arranged two above one. The legend SANCTUS ERICUS SVEVORVM GOTHORVM REX SIGILLVM REGNI SVECIAE makes it clear that these are the arms of Sweden. They have finally been accepted to represent the country. Their number would appear to have no reference to the kingdom of the Swedes, the Goths and the Wends.

In 1446 King Karl Knutsson Bonde used a seal which shows what one might describe as the prototype of the present-day Greater State Arms. The quarters represent the three crowns and the Folkunga Arms and are separated by a narrow cross. This was probably inspired by the arrangement outlined above, for over all he placed an escutcheon of the arms of Bonde. This pattern has remained in use ever since, succeeding dynasties merely changing the arms upon the inescutcheon. The arms of Vasa replaced those of Bonde, and Karl XIV Johan (1818–44) impaled his own arms of Bernardotte with the arms of Vasa, doubtless to indicate that he had been adopted as heir by the last sovereign of that House.

Sweden admirably illustrates the resolution of the initial uncertainty which has prevailed in many States with regard to their arms. To this day the State Arms of

Sweden occur in two principal forms—the Greater and the Lesser. The shield of the latter bears simply the three crowns.

From the foregoing it should be reasonably clear that even the most drastic changes in National Arms are made for a good and sufficient reason. By and large, after the early medieval period, one can see that even in the face of the most violent upheavals there is a deep-rooted desire to maintain some degree of continuity in the armorial display of the State. There is, furthermore, a desire to indicate the full extent of that State and, to that end, a sovereign may include quarterings for all those States which he claims to represent. Quarterings may also be introduced for reasons connected solely with his House. We have already observed the practice adopted by some sovereigns of placing the arms of their House in a smaller shield upon the arms of their State. A glance at the Royal Arms of Spain as borne by Alphonso XIII or the original version of the Royal Arms of Leopold I of Belgium will prove that the reverse procedure could also be adopted. In reality the presence of an inescutcheon does not necessarily indicate an elected sovereign, although it may do so; it is merely a convenient way of allying the arms of the monarch and of the State. The two most complicated royal coats in Europe today, those of Denmark and Greece, are very closely related. Denmark shows a complex arrangement of arms marshalled on a single shield together with the Cross of the Dannebrog. Upon this is placed another shield bearing yet a third. These indicate that the King of Denmark is a scion of the House of Oldenburg. The Royal Arms of Greece go one stage further; over the Greek National Arms is placed a shield of the complete arms of King Christian IX of Denmark whose son was raised to the Greek throne as George I.

In the nineteenth century several new monarchies were founded. Their arms followed traditional patterns. To Belgium and Greece we have already alluded, but the case of the Netherlands is of interest because of the way in which the arms of the reigning House were modified to form those of the State; the lion of Nassau was made to hold a sword and a bundle of arrows. Of course, not all European States are kingdoms. They include the Grand Duchy of Luxembourg and the Principalities of Liechtenstein and Monaco, all of which display typically dynastic arms. The Co-Principality of the Valleys of Andorra has two versions of its arms which recall its original joint suzerains, the Spanish Bishop of Urgel and the French Count of Foix. The older states also include the Swiss Confederation and the Republic of San Marino. The former gained practical independence of the Holy Roman Empire in 1499 and formal independence in 1648, yet its arms were only formally decreed in 1814.

This does not mean, however, that their history is so brief. Legend has it that in the most remote times red was the national colour of the first Scandinavian colonists who came to inhabit the high Alpine valleys; their banners and clothes were of this colour. In the most ancient times the white cross was carried by Swiss warriors on their clothes and flags since the freeing of their native land was regarded by them as a Crusade in itself. The Swiss Arms are mentioned for the first time in 1339 with reference to the Swiss forces leaving Berne to march against the army of nobles. 'And they were all marked with the sign of the Holy Cross, a white cross on a red shield . . .' says the chronicle of Justinger. It will be seen then how appropriately the Diet decreed in 1814: 'Seeing that it was the military sign of the ancient Swiss, the red shield carrying a white cross will compose the communal federal arms of the Confederation.' Such is the origin of the coat-of-arms which, by reversal of the colours, gave birth to the international sign of the Red Cross. The arms of the other European republic, San Marino, display its three castle-topped mountain peaks.

Europe also contains the smallest sovereign State in the world. This is also unique. It is the State of the City of the Vatican, over which His Holiness the Pope rules as sovereign. Guaranteed sovereignty as a State by the Lateran Treaty in 1929, it employs the Arms of the Holy See: the Papal Tiara and the Keys of St Peter.

Outside Europe, as already indicated, heraldry is derivative. It has spread by means of European influence and, more often than not, that influence has been colonial in character. Although a sovereign may include virtually any arms he may choose upon his shield, there must inevitably come a time when it is no longer practicable to add more. At the height of the British Empire it would clearly have been impossible to include upon a single shield all the territories represented by the Crown. The Crown very wisely made no attempt to do so. It was, nevertheless, desirable that the sovereign should be able to indicate his sovereignty in an armorial fashion. This was achieved by means of formally assigning arms for various colonies. This practice became widespread, and arms were granted for colonies, dominions and their constituent states and provinces.

Once the concept of sovereignty expressed armorially had become accepted abroad it was only natural that as countries which had been colonies attained independence they should continue the tradition. Of course, not all the arms then adopted followed traditional patterns but the intention was clear. On 4 July 1776 the British colonies in the southern part of North America formally declared their independence. The subsequent events must be too well known to readers to require repetition here. After long and fruitless discussion, the Continental Congress, on 20 June 1782, approved the design for what was to be the Great Seal of the United States of America. This was the work of many hands, but the design of the obverse was largely the suggestion of William Barton of Philadelphia. Had he been guided exclusively by European precedents he would doubtless have proposed a complex array of thirteen or so separate coats-of-arms marshalled upon a single shield. Deficient in expertise as the official blazon, i.e. formal heraldic description, undoubtedly is, the symbolism of the design is little short of a stroke of genius. All American readers will be fully aware of the nature of the design but, for the sake of British and other readers, we will take a closer look at it. The basic problem was to typify a union in one nation of thirteen constituents each preserving its individuality. The solution was as follows. A shield was made to consist of thirteen vertical red and white stripes united by a single blue band above them. This shield was then placed upon the breast of the American eagle (*Haliaetus leucocephalus*) which held in one claw a single branch of olive (for peace) and in the other thirteen arrows. In the beak was a ribbon inscribed 'E pluribus unum' (Out of many, one). Above the head were set thirteen silver stars 'forming a constellation' (in reality conforming to the general outline of a single six-pointed star) on a blue background surrounded by a glory breaking through the could. This design is essentially very simple, but how inspiring is its symbolism! It surely requires neither explanation nor apology.

Unhappily, other new sovereign States did not fare so well with the design of their newly acquired ensigns. Simple they may be, but they scarcely belong to the realms of heraldry. It would be both invidious and not a little unwise to single out any for special attention in this context, but a glance at the plates will enable the reader to draw his or her own conclusions. For the most part new States have tended to try to include within the confines of their shields a miscellany of articles which they have considered to be particularly appropriate to them. Some outstandingly beautiful designs have been produced in what might be regarded as the most unlikely places; in other countries such ineptness has been manifest that popular outcry has led to their replacement. The reader must not think that this stricture is confined to countries without a heraldic tradition. He must remember that the original arms of both the Commonwealth of Australia and the Dominion of Canada have been replaced because they were considered not entirely appropriate. No doubt there are other countries which are equally dissatisfied but have not ventured to express such an opinion.

We have not the space to include here a detailed account of the origin and development of the National Arms of every State which uses them; nor would the reader derive a great deal of benefit were we to do so. We still have much ground to cover and an entirely different category of devices to consider.

In the world today monarchies are decidedly in a minority, so that it is equally certain that the dynastic considerations which so often have governed the choice of arms for a State no longer have their former importance. Of course, not all monarchies have made use of arms; several stand completely outside the Western tradition. In some cases, however, there is a superficial resemblance due, as in the case of Ethiopia and Jordan, to the presence of what appears to be a pavilion. As the reader will have gathered, many States make use of emblems. These should not be dismissed lightly, because they are becoming increasingly prevalent among the new States. But from the historical point of view one can say that the most important factor in the decision to adopt an emblem rather than a more normal armorial arrangement is the desire to forget a past with unpleasant memories and begin anew.

The year 1789 is of great historical importance for in that year the French monarchy was overthrown and the existing order was swept away. The use of heraldic insignia was proscribed and the fleurs-de-lys were replaced by the tricolour. To this day the tricolour remains the only emblem of the French Republic, although the Third Republic approved the use of a different emblem which is still in use. In many parts of the world the discontent with existing regimes was brought to a head and within a few years revolution was rife. As each former colony gained its independence the new government adopted a device to represent the State and in so doing usually took great care to ignore its former masters.

We have already seen how the United States of America solved the problem; other American republics found far more dramatic solutions. Some of them adopted heraldic devices, but the majority cast heraldry aside and adopted emblems which were simultaneously vehicles for the expression of protest and of affirmation of their newly acquired sovereign independence. And so it has proceeded to the present day. As regime has succeeded regime the State Emblem has been changed and a new expression of the nation has been manifest. The modern genre of State Emblems provides too great a variety to admit of easy analysis, but it will be appreciated that National State Emblems have become far more than an expression of national solidarity and identity. They have become vehicles for political, social and ideological propaganda. For those with an intellect capable of comprehension, the symbols of the earthly powers are possessed of and invested with far deeper significance than their superficial appearance might suggest. 'Things more excellent than any symbol are expressed through symbols.' Men declare themselves in many ways; let us make the effort to understand them.

Independent States
as at 1st January 1971

Afghanistan
Albania

Algeria
Andorra

Arab Republic of Egypt
Argentina

Australia
Austria

Bahrain
Barbados

Belgium
Bhutan

Bolivia
Botswana

Brazil
Bulgaria

Burma
Burundi

Cambodia
Cameroon

Canada
Central African Republic

Ceylon
Chad

Chile
China (Communist)

China (Nationalist)
Colombia

Congo (Brazzaville)
Congo (Kinshasa)

Costa Rica
Cuba

Cyprus
Czechoslovakia

Dahomey
Denmark

Dominican Republic
Ecuador

Equatorial Guinea
Ethiopia

Fiji
Finland

France
Gabon

The Gambia
Germany (East)

Germany (West)
Ghana

Greece
Guatemala

Guinea
Guyana

Haiti	Mexico
Honduras	Monaco
Hungary	Mongolia
Iceland	Morocco
India	Muscat & Oman
Indonesia	Nauru
Iran	Nepal
Iraq	Netherlands
Ireland	New Zealand
Israel	Nicaragua
Italy	Niger
Ivory Coast	Nigeria
Jamaica	Norway
Japan	Pakistan
Jordan	Panama
Kenya	Paraguay
Korea (North)	Peru
Korea (South)	The Philippines
Kuwait	Poland
Laos	Portugal
Lebanon	Rhodesia
Lesotho	Romania
Liberia	Rwanda
Libya	El Salvador
Liechtenstein	San Marino
Luxembourg	Saudi Arabia
Madagascar	Senegal
Malawi	Sierra Leone
Malaysia	Singapore
The Maldives	Somalia
Mali	South Africa
Malta	Southern Yemen
Mauritania	Spain
Mauritius	Sudan

Swaziland
Sweden

Switzerland
Syria

Tanzania
Thailand

Togo
Tonga

Trinidad and Tobago
Tunisia

Turkey
Uganda

Union of Soviet Socialist
   Republics
United Kingdom

United States of America
Upper Volta

Uruguay
Vatican City

Venezuela
Vietnam (North)

Vietnam (South)
Western Samoa

Yemen
Yugoslavia

Zambia

1st September 1971
Qatar

National Heraldry of the World

AFGHANISTAN (Afghánistán). Kingdom of Afghanistan (Doulat I Pádsháhi Ye Afghánistán).
United in 1747 by Ahmed Shah Abdali, the country was for much of the nineteenth and
early twentieth centuries strongly influenced by Great Britain, which formally recognized
its complete independence in 1921. In 1926 the emirate became a kingdom, but this fell
into jeopardy in 1929 at the time of the Water Boy's Revolt; the capital, Kabul, was taken
and the monarchy overthrown. This revolt was, however, put down within the year by
Mohammed Nadir Khan who became the new monarch. The country is largely a tribal
society with an agricultural economy, the people being Moslem. The State Emblem has,
since about 1890, been a stylized picture of an open mosque with a praying recess and
pulpit; to this was added, in the 1920s, a wreath of wheat symbolizing agriculture and the
national unity. The wreath also refers to the tradition that the monarch was chosen in 1747
at a tribal council at which one of the army officers present was 'crowned' with such a
wreath by a dervish; he it was who became the sovereign. The date below the mosque
(1348) corresponds to the Gregorian year 1929 and has particular reference to the
restoration of the monarchy; the ribbon at the base of the wreath is inscribed 'Afghanistan'.
There are no official colours for the Emblem but it appears upon both the National Flag
and the Royal Standard in white; elsewhere the flags which flank the mosque are often
shown as the national tricolour.

ALBANIA (Shqiperia). The Albanian People's Republic (Republika Popullóre e Shqipërisë).
Throughout its history Albania has been subject to external pressures and has passed
through many hands. Incorporated into the Roman Empire in the first century A.D., it
passed into the Eastern Empire in 395; by the fourteenth century most of it had been
conquered by the Serbs, after which it was ruled by a succession of native princes until the
Turks began their conquests. Independence came once more in 1912; in 1914 the country
became a principality, in 1925 a republic, and in 1928 it became a kingdom. In 1939 it was
united to the Italian Crown but it became independent once again 29 November 1944. The
present People's Republic was officially proclaimed 11 January 1946 but is held to have
been formed at the Permet Congress on 24 May 1944, a date which is inscribed upon the
ribbon of the State Emblem. Since independence the Emblem of Albania has constantly
been the eagle, in allusion to the native name of the country which means 'The Land of
Eagles'. It also refers to the great Albanian patriot Skanderbeg and as such is an assertion
of national independence. The Emblem was adopted in its present form in 1945 and consists
of the eagle within the typically Communist framework of a star-topped wreath of grain
with a ribbon at the base, in this case bearing the date of the formation of the present
republic.

ALGERIA (El Djeza'ir; Algérie). The People's Democratic Republic of Algeria (El Djoumhouriyya el Djezairiyya ach Cha'biyya ed Dimukratiyya; République Algérienne Démocratique et Populaire).

This country, before achieving independence on 3 July 1962, had long been under foreign rule. Conquered by the Arabs in the seventh century, it was from 1518 ruled by the Turks; in 1830 the French occupied Algeria, and annexed it in 1842. The fifteen Algerian departments of Metropolitan France became independent after a bloody war and, as is not unusual in such cases, chose not to make any reference in the new State Emblem to the immediate past. Instead they sought to epitomize an Islamic republic by incorporating National Flags with the Star and Crescent. In the flags the white is said to stand for purity whilst the green is alleged to have been the Prophet's favourite colour. In fact green, white, black and red are characteristic colours in Islam and the different interpretations which may be placed upon them are infinite. It will be observed that the horns of the crescent are somewhat longer than is customary; this is held to bring better luck. Among other features incorporated in the Emblem is the hand of Fatima, the youngest daughter of Mohammed and ancestress of the Fatimid rulers of North Africa; in Moslem countries this is regarded as the symbol of happiness.

ANDORRA (Andorra; Andorre). The Valleys of Andorra (Las Valls d'Andorra; Les Vallées d'Andorre).

Tradition has it that Charlemagne guaranteed, in 784, that the people of Andorra could live in freedom; in 843 the Emperor Charles II appointed the Count of Urgel its overlord. From this family the rights passed, by inheritance, to the French Comte de Foix with whom, by the Paréage of 1278, the Catalan Bishop of Urgel was made joint suzerain. The rights of the count passed via the House of Albret to King Henri IV of France and from the monarchs to the French presidents. At the present time the Bishop of Urgel and the President of the French Republic are co-princes, France taking care of the country's relations with others. The co-principality has always maintained virtual independence, even to the extent of a trial period (in 1806) as a republic, and today pays homage to its suzerains only through nominal annual payments. The State Coat-of-Arms, perhaps because there are two princes, occurs in two distinct forms; that which we illustrate, being the one to appear on the State Flag, is the Spanish version. The French version is not often seen and differs only in the arrangement of the crozier and mitre. These refer to the Bishop of Urgel; the three red stripes refer to the Comte de Foix; the four red stripes refer to Catalonia; the two cows refer to the Comte de Béarn. The coronet is that appropriate to a French count and the motto may be translated 'Strength is increased by unity'.

4

VIRTUS UNITA FORTIOR

THE ARAB REPUBLIC OF EGYPT (Al Djumhuriyey al-'Arabîye al Misr).
This State is undoubtedly better known as Egypt and it is unnecessary to dwell upon its past, but its official title requires some explanation. The country became independent in 1922 and became a kingdom; following a coup in 1952 a republic was established on 18 June 1953. The United Arab Republic was formed on 1 February 1958 when Syria was joined with Egypt. On 8 March 1958 the Republic of the Yemen also joined the confederation but this soon came to an end; Syria withdrew on 30 September 1961 and the Yemen on 26 December 1961. In spite of this the name was retained. The State Coat-of-Arms was adopted in 1958 on the formation of the United Arab Republic and it is the key to the many other State Coats-of-Arms of similar form. The eagle is 'Saladin's eagle' and bears on its breast a shield derived from the National Flag; beneath the eagle and held in its talons is a plaque inscribed with the name of the country in Kufic script. The two stars represent Egypt and Syria which together formed the United Republic.

ARGENTINA. The Argentine Republic (República Argentina).
This country was first discovered in 1515 and was gradually colonized by Spain in the succeeding century; independence from the mother country was finally achieved in 1816, being declared on 9 July at the Congress of Tucuman. The State Emblem was adopted in 1813 during the war of independence and is full of significance. When Spain and Great Britain were at war (1806–7) the British invaded Argentina and tried to capture Buenos Aires; one of the volunteer groups formed in the city to resist the attack chose light blue and white as its colours, which became symbolic of Argentine patriotism. Such were the ribbons being handed out in the city square on 25 May 1810 when the patriots were assembled to demand freedom from Spain. The day was stormy; presently news came that the Spanish viceroy had resigned, and at that moment, according to legend, the sun burst through the clouds and shone down on the assembly. This was interpreted as an auspicious omen. All this is indicated in the Emblem, which is clearly inspired by the symbolism of the French Revolution. The two clasped hands (of fraternity and unity) grasp a staff which is surmounted by a red cap of liberty; the oval of the national colours is surrounded by the laurels of victory and the 'Sun of May' looks down on all. The theme is one of fraternity and equality in unified liberty.

AUSTRALIA. The Commonwealth of Australia.

The Commonwealth of Australia was officially inaugurated on 1 January 1901 and now comprises, in addition to the Federal Capital Territory, the States of Western Australia, South Australia, Queensland, New South Wales, Tasmania and Victoria; it also includes the Northern Territory and the Territory of Papua and New Guinea. Each of the constituent states has its own Arms, yet, although those of the Commonwealth symbolize the union of six states, there is little obvious resemblance; in fact the Commonwealth Arms, which were granted by Royal Warrant 19 September 1912 to replace an earlier achievement in response to popular demand, indicate the several states by means of their flag badges. These are grouped together as quarterings on a shield and a semblance of unity is given to the whole by the addition of a border. The seven-pointed star of the crest is known as the 'Commonwealth Star' and refers to the constituents at the time of the grant. The supporters, a kangaroo and an emu, are characteristic of the continent as is also the wattle (the national flower) upon a background of which the arms are frequently displayed.

AUSTRIA (Österreich). Republic of Austria (Republik Österreich).

In spite of its long history, Austria emerged as a sovereign independent state divorced from all others only with the downfall of the Austro-Hungarian monarchy in 1918. The Republic of German Austria was proclaimed 12 November 1918 and in November 1920 became a federal republic of eight provinces (increased to nine by the addition of Vienna in 1922). This republic fell to Nazi Germany in 1938; after the Second World War the country passed under Allied occupation and, although the Austrian State was revived in 1945, it was not re-established as an independent Sovereign State until 1955. The new State adopted, 1 May 1945, in accordance with the Law of Coats of Arms Art. 1, para. 2, a new State Coat-of-Arms based upon that of the old republic of 1918. The imperial eagle, having on its head a mural crown (for the burghers) and grasping in its talons a sickle and hammer (for farmers and artisans), has broken fetters on its legs specifically referring to the liberation of 1945 and to distinguish it from the eagle of the earlier republic. Upon its breast is placed a shield of the Arms of the House of Babenburg which have for so long served for those of Austria.

AUSTRALIA

BAHRAIN. The State of Bahrain.

This Arab state consists of a group of islands in the Persian Gulf sheltered by the Qatar peninsula. From the time of the Shah Abbas I (1587–1628) until 1782 the islands were under the rule of Persia; in the last year Al-Khalifa ancestors of the present dynasty seized the government. From 1861 until independence was attained on 15 August 1971 Bahrain was under British protection, and from 30 March 1968 formed a part of the Federation of Arab Emirates of the Persian Gulf. The State Arms, which were designed by the sheik's political adviser, Sir Charles Belgrave, are derived from the design of the State Flag which was adopted in 1932. The original flag was completely red, as is usual in the Persian Gulf, but later a white band (usually with an indented edge) was added in the hoist to distinguish this flag from those of other Arab States. The Arms show fewer indentations than does the Flag and the Arms are sometimes surmounted by a crown.

BARBADOS.

This, the most easterly and most densely populated of the West Indian Islands, was first settled by Great Britain in 1627. It derives its name, given to it by the Portuguese, from its 'bearded' fig-trees. The island was granted internal self-government by the mother country in 1961 and achieved full independence as a member of the British Commonwealth of Nations on 30 November 1966. The State Coat-of-Arms, which was granted in 1965, displays the *Ficus barbata*, after which the island is named, accompanied by two orchids. The crest consists of a native arm holding two sticks of sugar cane and the shield is supported by a dolphin and a pelican. The whole indicates something of the island's resources as expressed in the motto 'Pride and Industry'.

10

PRIDE AND INDUSTRY

BELGIUM (Belgique; België). The Kingdom of Belgium (Royaume de Belgique; Koninkrijk België).

In the fifteenth century modern Belgium consisted of a number of feudal states united under the Duchy of Burgundy, from which they passed to the House of Habsburg; by the Treaty of Campo Formio, 1797, they were transferred from Austria to France, only to be transferred once more, by the Treaty of Paris in 1815, to the Netherlands. In 1830 revolution broke out in Brussels and independence was proclaimed on 14 October of that year. In 1831 Leopold of Saxe-Coburg-Saalfeld was chosen King of the Belgians and adopted a most unusual type of Royal Arms. As husband of the daughter of the British Prince Regent (afterwards King George IV) he had been granted the right to combine a version of the British Royal Arms with those of his own House; this he did by quartering the two. As King of the Belgians he broke with all precedent by adopting the irregular expedient of placing upon these Arms those of his newly acquired kingdom. Many examples of this curious arrangement are known, but a Royal Decree dated 13 July 1880 finally placed the Arms of Belgium (the lion of Brabant) directly upon the shield, the Arms of Saxony being placed over them on a smaller shield. After the First World War the Arms of Saxony were dropped, leaving the Arms as they appear today. The shield is surrounded by the Collar of the Order of Leopold and is supported by two lions bearing banners in the form of the National Flag, the colours of which refer to the three regions (Flanders, Wallonia, and Brabant) which make up the country. The motto means 'Unity gives strength' and is usually, as here, given in French; it may however be found in Flemish ('Eendracht Maakt Macht') or in both languages together.

BHUTAN (Druk-Yul). Kingdom of Bhutan (Druk Gyalkhap).

This little country is a bone of contention between the republics of India and China; for one of them directs its foreign affairs whilst the other regards it as part of greater Tibet. The country's inhabitants are, in fact, ethnically related to the Tibetans, though in the past Mongols and Indians have added to the strain. The dominant religion is Mahayana Buddhism, which is a form closely related to Tibetan Lamaism. Tibet conquered Bhutan in the sixteenth century and it was largely because of Great Britain's activities that the country became a hereditary monarchy in 1907. The title of the monarch is the Thunder King or the Dragon King and the Tibetan name for the country signifies the 'Realm of the Dragon'. In fact the word for dragon, *druk*, can also mean thunder. In Asia the dragon symbolizes power and magnanimity. The State Emblem consists of two dragons supporting a flame and guarding a thunderbolt in the form of a cross.

12

ROYAL GOVERNMENT OF BHUTAN

BOLIVIA. Republic of Bolivia (República de Bolivia; *or* República Boliviana).
The rich silver mines of this high cold country, discovered as early as 1545, attracted the
Spanish who ruled until 1825, victory for the patriots under de Sucre coming in 1824 at
Ayachuco. The Arms were adopted by law 14 July 1888 and are modelled on an earlier
State Emblem dating from 1825. They depict a landscape with the sun shining over Mount
Potosí, near which were the Indian silver mines; also included are an alpaca, a house, a
breadfruit tree, and a sheaf of grain. The whole symbolizes the riches of the country,
mineral, vegetable and animal. The stars on the border correspond in number to the
departments forming the country, and behind the oval appear two crossed cannon and four
rifles (with bayonets fixed), six tricolour flags, a cap of liberty, and a battle-axe. The last
stands for the Inca Indians who ruled much of the country long ago. Above the cartouche
is a condor between a branch of laurel and a branch of olive. The theme of natural riches
is echoed in the tricolour flags in which red represents the animals, yellow the minerals
and green the plants and trees.

BOTSWANA. Republic of Botswana.
Bechuanaland, as this country was called in its days as a British protectorate, was first
visited by missionaries in the nineteenth century, yet it attracted little European attention.
Under Chief Khama a fairly unified State was developed and he it was, when the Boers of
the Transvaal threatened his territory, who requested Great Britain's protection. The
country became fully independent as a member of the British Commonwealth of Nations on
30 September 1966. In the Arms the rust-coloured bull's head refers to the cattle industry;
the cogwheels symbolize racial harmony, co-operation between the tribes, and the country's
budding industry; the sorghum (millet) refers to agriculture, whilst the two zebras and the
elephant's tusk indicate the fauna of the country. The principal reason for the choice of the
zebra was that it is a truly neutral animal, since it is not the totem of any tribe; its black
and white colouring, too, symbolizes the inhabitants of the state—both black and white—
as one people. The wavy blue lines point to the country's reliance upon water which is its
very life-blood, a point further emphasized by the motto, which signifies 'Rain'.

BRAZIL (Brasil). The Federative Republic of Brazil (República Federativa do Brasil).
By far the largest of the Latin American countries, Brazil is unique among them in that its language is Portuguese; this is due to its lying within the Portuguese sphere of influence as defined in the Treaty of Tordesillas of 1494. The country was formally claimed for Portugal in 1500. Declared independent as an empire on 7 September 1822, a bloodless revolution established a republic which was proclaimed on 15 November 1889. Shortly afterwards the State Emblem was adopted, certain details being altered in 1968. The State Emblem offers an interesting example of non-armorial display which, however, gives the immediate impression of the star of a Chivalric Order. This star is five-pointed with each point parted in green and yellow, the whole being edged in red and yellow and set upon golden rays. These colours are significant of the natural resources, as in the case of Bolivia. The star bears a representation of the constellation of the Southern Cross within a circlet bearing twenty-two stars (one for each of the constituent states). The great star itself represents unity and independence and is set upon a naked sword and a chaplet of coffee and tobacco leaves to indicate the staple crops. The ribbon beneath the emblem bears the country's name and the date of the proclamation of the republic.

BULGARIA (Bulgarija). The People's Republic of Bulgaria (Narodna Republika Bălgarija).
From 681, until its annexation by the Byzantine Empire in 1018, Bulgaria was itself an empire. In 1186 it became independent once again only to fall, via the status of a tributary to Serbia, into absorption by the Ottoman Empire in 1396. Independence was not again achieved until 1908, although the Treaty of Berlin in 1878 had made North Bulgaria a tributary principality under Turkish suzerainty. In 1908 the Prince proclaimed Bulgarian independence with himself as Tsar. In 1946 a People's Republic was proclaimed and this retained the lion of the old Royal Arms when selecting the new State Emblem. The golden lion was placed above a cogwheel on a blue field within the usual Communist wreath of wheat and star. The date on the ribbon is that of the *coup d'état* of the Fatherland Front which brought about the republic.

BURMA (Myanma). The Republic of the Burmese Union (Pyee-Daung-Su Myanma-Nainggan-Daw).
The history of Burma is a succession of unification, disintegration and reunification until 1758 when final unity was achieved. It was, thereafter, annexed piecemeal by the British, who made it a dependency of India. The British did much to develop the country's natural resources, but growing dissatisfaction led to separation from India in 1937 and, as far as internal affairs were concerned, Burma gained the equivalent of dominion status. After Japanese occupation during the war, Burma obtained complete independence from Britain and elected to withdraw from the British Commonwealth; the Union of Burma was set up as a republic on 4 January 1948, thus completing the movement initiated in 1937 and interrupted in 1942. The State Coat-of-Arms displays on a round shield a map of the country enclosed in a red scroll whose inscription means 'Happiness and prosperity through unity'. The Burmese Lions—the 'Chinthe', those fabulous beasts of Burmese mythology which were regarded as the guardians of sacred treasure—guard the shield; below the whole is another scroll bearing the name of the country. The number three is considered to be a lucky one. It will be recalled that the troops popularly known as the 'Chindits' derived their name from these beasts.

BURUNDI (Burundi). Republic of Burundi (Republika y'Uburundi; République de Burundi).
The healthful plateau region of Ruanda-Burundi was occupied in ancient times by a pygmy people who were gradually driven into the forests by Bantu infiltration. In the fifteenth and sixteenth centuries there came a further infiltration of the Watutsi, those warriors of great stature, who formed two kingdoms in Ruanda and Burundi. The interior was first penetrated by a European in 1894 and soon after the two kingdoms were incorporated into German East Africa. After the First World War the territory became a Belgian League of Nations mandated territory, which was changed in 1946 to a United Nations trust territory. On 1 July 1962 the country split when the Republic of Rwanda and the Kingdom of Burundi gained independence as separate states, the latter electing for a republican form of government in 1966, the formal proclamation taking place on 23 November. The State Coat-of-Arms is of the very simplest description; the motto means 'Unity, Work, Progress'.

CAMBODIA (Kampuchea; Cambodge). The Khmer Republic.

From being the dominant state (as the Khmer Empire) in south-east Asia, Cambodia had sunk so far by 1854 that the king appealed to France for intervention; in 1865 a French protectorate was established, that country's influence being consolidated by a treaty in 1884. It became part of the Union of Indo-China in 1887 and was subject to Japanese occupation in the Second World War, after which France granted it a greater degree of self-government within the the Federation of Indo-China. In May 1947 Cambodia became a constitutional monarchy and on 8 November 1949 it became an associated state within the French Union. In 1953 it declared itself independent, although France did not transfer full sovereignty until December 1954. The country finally left the French Union on 25 September 1955 and became a republic on 9 October 1970. The new republic does not yet appear finally to have adopted a new State Emblem, but in the absence of details we illustrate that of the former kingdom. It is known that the motto will be 'Liberty, Equality, Fraternity, Progress, Happiness'. The Royal Arms of Cambodia included goblets, sword and a crown with rays in token of the king's power and dignity. The lions supporting the Emblem were added in 1951 and are somewhat unusual, the left-hand one having an elephant's head; they are symbols of authority and strength. Each holds a five-tiered umbrella, the south-east Asian symbol of supremacy and power.

CAMEROUN. Federal Republic of Cameroun (République Fédérale du Cameroun).

In early times the region was dominated by a succession of many invaders and came under German control in the late nineteenth century, possession being recognized in 1902. In 1911 part of French Equatorial Africa was added but this was withdrawn again after the First World War. In 1919 the remainder of the Cameroons were divided into a British and a French zone which became at first mandates under the League of Nations and later trust territories of the United Nations. On 1 January 1960 the French Cameroons, which had been granted self-government in 1957 and internal autonomy in 1959, became the Cameroon Republic which, upon the addition of the southern section of the British Cameroons in 1961, subsequently became the Federal Republic of Cameroun. The State Coat-of-Arms bears a conventionalized map of the country, a balance and two stars, and the shield is placed upon two fasces. The shield varies with respect to colours, but the red inverted 'pile' represents Mount Cameroun and its colour represents the power uniting the two parts of the federation (which are themselves indicated by the two stars); the green symbolizes the vegetation of the south and the hope of a happy future; the yellow symbolizes the wealth of the north and the sun. The sword and balance represent political equality and unity, while the fasces represent the authority of the State. Occasionally a motto 'Paix, Travail, Patrie' (Peace, Work, Fatherland) is used.

CANADA. Dominion of Canada.

As everyone is well aware Canada was, ignoring the somewhat obscure activities of the Vikings after A.D. 1000, settled by the British and French in rivalry. The country has developed from a number of separate colonies which have come together in the course of time. The dominion was brought about by the British North America Act of 1867 and came into being on 1 July 1867, thus making Canada the oldest of the independent Commonwealth countries. Total independence in all fields was not attained however until 12 December 1931. The Dominion at present comprises the Provinces of British Columbia, Manitoba, New Brunswick, Newfoundland, Nova Scotia, Prince Edward Island, Quebec and Saskatchewan, with the Yukon and North West Territories. Each of these has its own arms and, indeed, the very first Dominion Arms consisted of the quartered coats of Ontario, Quebec, Nova Scotia and New Brunswick. This arrangement did not, however, prove satisfactory and new arms were assigned by Royal Proclamation on 21 November 1921. The new design indicated the British and French contribution by means of the Royal Heraldry of the two countries, while representing Canada as a whole by the maple leaf. The extent of the country is indicated in the motto 'From sea to sea'.

CENTRAL AFRICAN REPUBLIC. (République Centrafricaine.)

This was formerly the territory of Ubangi-Shari in French Equatorial Africa. It was first settled by the French in 1887 and by them organized as a colony in 1894. United administratively with Chad in 1906, it was incorporated into French Equatorial Africa in 1910. During the 1950s the colony gained increasingly greater autonomy and in December 1958 became the Central African Republic within the French Community. Final and complete independence was attained 13 August 1960. The symbolism of the State Coat-of-Arms is not altogether clear; clearly the elephant and tree represent the country's fauna and flora, and the hand appears to point to the map of Africa which is surmounted by a star indicative of African liberty. The star may also point to a state in Central Africa. The motto above the shield may be roughly translated 'All men are equal'; that below means 'Unity, Dignity, Work'. These arms were adopted in 1963.

CEYLON. Dominion of Ceylon.
The most ancient inhabitants of this island seem to have been the ancestors of the Veddas, an aboriginal people. In the sixth century B.C. they were conquered by the Singhalese, who later had to resist many Tamil invasions. In this they were not too successful, since the country came to have both Singhalese and Tamil kingdoms. In the sixteenth century European influence began to be felt; first of all came the Portuguese, who conquered the coastal areas; by the mid seventeenth century their place had been taken by the Dutch who, in 1795, were displaced by the British, who made the island a Crown Colony in 1798. The island was unified for the very first time in 1815 when the Kingdom of Kandy, which formed the central part of the island, was conquered. During the First World War a movement for independence arose and this received final satisfaction at the attainment of full independence as a dominion within the British Commonwealth on 4 February 1948. The Arms, which were granted (without specifying the colours) on 30 July 1954, refer back to the Kingdom of Kandy and include the well-known Sinhaladipa or Ceylonese lion within a border of lotus petals which is symbolic of the nation. The inscription on the motto scroll gives the island's name in Singhalese (Lanka), Tamil (Ilange) and English (Ceylon). The colours of the ribbon, which appear also in the flag, represent the three principal races of the island. The roundel is surmounted by the crown of Kandy.

CHAD (Tchad). Republic of Chad (République du Tchad).
British explorers first entered this region in 1822 and were followed in 1890 by the French, who in 1900 defeated Rabah Amorey, the last of the Africans to oppose French conquest. The area was organized as a colony and became part of French Equatorial Africa. Later it was administratively linked with Ubangi-Shari (*see* Central African Republic), but it again became a separate colony in 1920. It became a republic within the French Community in 1958, full independence being achieved on 11 August 1960. There are no State Arms, but the State Seal, here illustrated, bears the head of a young woman, whose hair is elaborately dressed with plaits. In the border appear the name of the country and the motto 'Unity, Work, Progress'.

CHILE. Republic of Chile (República de Chile).

During most of the colonial period Chile was a captaincy general dependent on the viceroyalty of Peru, but in 1778 it became a separate division. Its boundaries were then ill-defined and this gave rise, after independence, to protracted boundary disputes with neighbouring countries. The movement towards independence from Spain began in 1810, and independence was finally proclaimed by Bernardo O'Higgins on 12 February 1818. The State Coat-of-Arms was adopted in 1834 and consists of a white star (representing by its colour the snow of the high Andean mountains) which guides the country towards honour and progress at the same time as it stands for the Indian minority of the population, set upon a field parted in red (for the blood shed by those who fought for independence) and blue (for the sky overhead). Above the shield are placed three feathers of the rhea in the national colours, the shield being supported by a huemal (or guemal), a furcuferine deer found only in the country's mountain ranges, and a condor of the type found in the Andes. The motto 'By right or might' was coined during the war of independence.

CHINA (Chung-kuo). People's Republic of China (Chung-hua Jen-min Kung-ho Kuo).

The ancient Chinese Empire, which had persisted for many centuries, finally fell; the Emperor abdicated in 1912. In that year a republic was proclaimed on 12 February; yet this Great Chinese Republic was to have its difficulties too. In 1912 the Chinese Communist Party was formed, and with it Sun Yat-Sen soon formed an alliance; his successor Chiang Kai-Shek, however, reversed his policy and in 1926 there began the long civil war between the Kuomintang and the Communists. The 'Long March' and its aftermath have long passed into history, but on 21 September 1949 the Communists had so gained ground that they proclaimed their rule over the whole of China; indeed, by August of that year Chiang had only the island of Taiwan (Formosa) in his possession. The State Emblem officially depicts the Gate of Heavenly Peace at Peking under the light of five stars within a wreath of ears of grain with a cogwheel at the base. This is a typical Communist emblem, though in this case the symbolism of the stars is rather more fully developed than is usual. The larger star represents the republic and its 'programme' (in other words, the leadership of the Party); the four smaller ones represent the four classes of the People's Republic upon whose support it relies: workers, peasants, petty bourgeoisie (i.e. small business men) and 'patriotic' capitalists. Another interpretation, equally valid, would assign them the classes of worker—agricultural, industrial, white-collar and managerial. The wreath, of course, represents agriculture, the cogwheel being for industrial development; the two together indicate the dichotomy of labour, the symbolism of the better-known hammer and sickle.

POR LA RAZON O LA FUERZA

CHINA (Chung-kuo). Republic of China (Chung-hua Min Kuo; *or* Ta Chung-hua Min-kuo).
Although, as indicated in the preceding article, Chiang Kai-Shek now holds only the island
of Taiwan (otherwise known as Formosa), the flag and emblem of the old republic continue
in use; in order to understand the symbolism we must consider them together. The colours,
red, blue and white, stand for what are called the Three Principles of the People: red stands
for liberty, sacrifice and nationalism; blue for equality, justice and democracy; white for
fraternity, frankness and the livelihood of the people. The emblem consists of a twelve-
rayed sun; in this the twelve points represent the twelve hours of a clock, the sun itself
being a symbol of progress. Thus one might summarize the emblem (which was originally
that of the Kuomintang Party) as representing continued progress through democratic
fraternity.

COLOMBIA. Republic of Colombia (República de Colombia).
This country was made a Spanish colony in 1536 and at its greatest extent included not
only the modern Colombia but also Ecuador, Panama and Venezuela. In 1564 it was
created a presidency loosely attached to the viceroyalty of Peru and in 1717 became the
viceroyalty of New Granada. Later the captaincy general of Venezuela and the presidency
of Quito were detached, thus creating a political division which withstood even Bolivar's
efforts to establish a Republic of Greater Colombia. The whole did in fact become
independent in 1819, but as a unit it soon fell apart. Colombia had proclaimed itself
independent on 20 July 1810 and the struggle to put its proclamation into effect took many
years. The new State which arose in 1819 began to disintegrate in 1830 when Venezuela and
Ecuador became separate States (or rather nations); the remaining territory emerged as the
Republic of New Granada. Subsequently the name was changed several times before it
became the Republic of Colombia. Panama itself seceded, with United States assistance,
in 1903. The State Coat-of-Arms goes back to the early days of independence and was
adopted in 1832; minor alterations were made in 1948 and 1955. Included within the shield
are the red cap of liberty, a pomegranate (for the name of New Granada), two cornucopias
(one dropping fruit, the other coins, to suggest riches) and a conventional representation of
the Pacific and Atlantic Oceans separated by the Isthmus of Panama, which was at that
time included within the boundaries. Behind the shield, which is upheld by an Andean
condor by means of a rope of laurel, appear four National Flags which are themselves
based upon those of the rebels.

CONGO (Brazzaville). People's Republic of the Congo (République Populaire du Congo).
For obvious reasons this and the next country are usually known by a name other than the official one; various popular names exist, but the easiest distinction is made by reference to their respective capitals which lie on opposite banks of the Congo River from which they both derive their official titles. Their names may be similar and their official language identical, but there the similarity ends; history distinguishes them. The one with which we now deal was in early times part of the African kingdom of the Congo. Under French influence originally called French Congo and later Middle Congo, it became in 1910 a colony in French Equatorial Africa. Having been granted internal autonomy in 1956 it became in 1958 a republic within the French Community and ultimately attained full independence on 15 August 1960. It has been a People's Republic since 31 December 1969. It would appear likely that the device upon the National Flag has become the new State Emblem. This would then be a circular design composed of two palm branches, the top being closed by a gold five-pointed star, the bottom enclosing a crossed hammer and hoe; and as such would be a novel variation of a well-known Communist theme. In the absence of confirmation, however, we illustrate the State Coat-of-Arms adopted in 1963. The lion with the torch of freedom symbolizes the Congolese nation and the green wavy bar symbolizes the River Congo. The 'forest crown' above the shield bears the name of the country and is a symbol of national sovereignty. The motto means 'Unity, Work, Progress'.

CONGO (Kinshasa). Democratic Republic of the Congo (République Démocratique du Congo).
Prior to independence this country was known as the Belgian Congo. Before that it was the Congo Free State and as such was organized by King Leopold II of the Belgians with himself as proprietor and sole monarch. In 1908, however, as a result of international protest against the prevailing abuses, it became a colony and its name was changed in accordance with its new status. After serious rioting a specific programme was agreed leading to immediate independence, this being formally proclaimed on 30 June 1960. The State Coat-of-Arms was adopted in 1963 and displays a leopard's head, palm branch, elephant's tusk and a crossed spear and arrow. The inscription, which appears inside the shield, means 'Justice, Peace, Work'.

COSTA RICA. Republic of Costa Rica (República de Costa Rica).
Spanish rule over this country began in 1563 and was exchanged for rule by Iturbide's Mexican Empire in 1821; from 1823 to 1838 it formed a part of the Central American Federation (then known as the United Provinces of Central America). Thus, although the country was nominally independent after 15 September 1821, it took some seventeen years to stand alone. After Francisco Morazán vainly tried to make the country the nucleus of a new federation, Costa Rica consistently opposed later efforts towards union. The present design of the Arms was adopted in 1964, but represents an alteration of the design of 1908, which is itself an adaptation of that of 1848; the theme is Costa Rica between the Caribbean and the Pacific. The shield displays two seas separated by three mountains and on each of the seas a ship is sailing; above the mountains there appear five stars. These stars allude to the former member States of the Federation, the arms of which were somewhat similar. The mountains in the present instance represent Mounts Barba, Irazu and Poás, while the seas indicate that the country has outlets to both the Pacific and Atlantic Oceans. The seas also symbolize the international nature of the country's trade.

CUBA. Republic of Cuba (República de Cuba).
This island was discovered by Christopher Columbus in 1492; by 1511 the Spanish had gained such a foothold that even in the early nineteenth century, when so much of the Spanish Empire was being transformed into new republics, Cuba remained firmly under Spanish control. This was due, however, to the fact that Cuban uprisings, which certainly did take place, were quickly crushed. Finally in 1895 a successful revolt broke out; following United States intervention the Spanish forces were defeated and a treaty, ratified in 1899, established the island as an independent republic under U.S. protection. This protection lasted until 1902 when U.S. military occupation ended; and so Cuban independence really dates from 20 May 1902. The State Coat-of-Arms, like the flag, was actually designed in 1849 long before independence; the designer was the poet Miguel Terbe Tolón, who was exiled with General Narciso López, the leader of the Cuban freedom movement. The Arms include the Cuban national colours in the form of blue and white stripes; the other half of the shield displays a landscape in which a royal palm (the most beautiful tree among the Cuban flora) is set in a valley between two mountains (representing the island). The seascape above represents the sun rising over a key set between two promontories. This indicates that Cuba (the key to the Gulf of Mexico) is set in the tropics (the sun) in the Caribbean (the sea) between the coasts of Florida and Yucatan (the promontories). The lictors' rods behind the shield stand for support and authority, the Phrygian cap and star being symbols of freedom, democracy and equality.

CYPRUS (Kipros; Kibris). Republic of Cyprus (Kipriaki Dimokratia; Kibris Cumhuriyeti).
This island has a long and colourful history; excavations have proved the existence of a
Neolithic culture in the fourth millennium B.C. Phoenicians settled there *circa* 800 B.C, and
it has been under Assyrian, Egyptian and Persian rule. The apostles Paul and Barnabas
introduced Christianity to the island, which was a centre of commerce. In 1191 Richard I
of England conquered it from the Byzantine Empire and gave it to the House of Lusignan;
in 1489 it was annexed to the Republic of Venice. In 1571 the Turks conquered it and in
1898 the Ottoman Empire placed the island under the protection of Great Britain, which
annexed it in 1914. It became a Crown Colony in 1925. Thereafter the movement for union
with Greece was a constant source of tension in the island which even independence has not
fully resolved. The island became an independent republic on 16 August 1960 and in the
following year it chose to become a member of the British Commonwealth of Nations. In
view of its troubled history it may appear surprising that the State Coat-of-Arms should
display the conventional emblem of Peace, the dove and olive branch, but the formation of
the republic was intended to bring peace to the two population groups (Greeks and Turks)
on the island. There can be no doubt that this is the intended meaning.

**CZECHOSLOVAKIA (Československo). Czechoslovak Socialist Republic (Československá
Socjalistická Repubiká).**
The history of the republic is short since it came into existence only in 1918; the history of
the land, however, is long. Essentially the republic is a union of the Czech lands with
Slovakia, both of which had been included in the old Austro-Hungarian Empire which
broke up in 1918. The present State Coat-of-Arms was set out in the constitution of July
1960 and embodied in a special law in November of that year. The shape of the shield
recalls the Hussite wars against the Holy Roman Empire, but it may have added
significance; the shape is characteristic of the pavisse, which was a large shield intended to
be set on the ground for the protection of infantry—it could therefore represent 'the shield
of the people'. Upon the shield is placed the lion of Bohemia, which dates from 1250 and
was adopted by Vladislav II. Upon its breast is a smaller shield showing the blue outline
of the Kriváň Mountain (one of the most typical mountains of Slovakia) overlaid by the
golden fire of freedom. Above the lion's head is the Communist star. On the President's
Standard these are displayed accompanied by a wreath of linden leaves and the motto
'Pravda vítězí' (Truth prevails).

DAHOMEY. Republic of Dahomey (République du Dahomey).

For a long time the land was divided into several small kingdoms, attaining unity only in the nineteenth century; in 1851 the King of Dahomey signed a trade agreement with the French, but difficulties with his successors led to military intervention and ultimate annexation in 1892. In 1904 the country was incorporated in French West Africa. In 1958 Dahomey became an autonomous state within the French Community and complete independence was achieved on 1 August 1960. The State Coat-of-Arms was adopted in 1964 and is an epitome of the country. The first quarter includes a *Somba* castle, the second displays the Badge of the Order of the Star of Benin, the third and fourth include a palm tree and a sailing ship respectively. The shield, which is supported by two leopards, is ensigned by two cornucopias which are somewhat unusual as the bounty which they provide consists of maize cobs. The motto means 'Fraternity, Justice, Work'.

DENMARK (Danmark). Kingdom of Denmark (Kongeriget Danmark).

This is a very old European monarchy and its rulers have, at various times, ruled over extensive empires including not only the Scandinavian peninsula but also England. The present Royal House of Denmark descends from the ducal House of Oldenburg which came to the Danish throne in 1448. The lion coat of Denmark is found in the twelfth century, but the complete achievement is the product of historical development; it virtually embodies the country's history among its many quarterings which at the present time include Denmark, Schleswig, Sweden, the Faroe Islands, Greenland, Gothland and Vandalia; the quarters are separated by the cross of the Dannebrog, over which is placed the Arms of the House of Oldenburg to indicate the kingly rights exercised by that House over the kingdom. This is always the true significance of these escutcheons, which have nothing to do with election. The Oldenburg Arms include those of Holstein, Stomarn, Ditzmarschen and Lauenburg, upon which are placed (once more as an assertion of rights) those of Oldenburg and Delmenhorst. This latest version of the complete achievement dates from 1948 and is based on the Arms of 1819; occasionally the motto 'Dominus mihi adiutor' (The Lord is a helper unto me) appears upon a ribbon behind the crown surmounting the mantle.

FRATERNITE JUSTICE TRAVAIL

DOMINUS MIHI ADIUTOR

DOMINICAN REPUBLIC (República Dominicana).

The whole island of Hispaniola was originally a Spanish colony which was known by the name of Santo Domingo. In 1677, however, the French seized the western part and made it a colony; this received the name Haiti. The eastern half was ceded to France in 1795, but was reoccupied by Spain in 1816; it declared its independence from Spain in 1821 and in the following year was subject to invasion from its neighbour, thereby losing its newly won freedom. The new regime, which sought to impose the French language, was overthrown in 1844 and since then continuous independence has been enjoyed. The State Coat-of-Arms, which was adopted in 1844, is substantially the same as the National Flag; both were designed by Juan Pablo Duarte, the founder of the *La Trinitaria* movement, which caused the country to break away from Haiti. The shield is divided exactly like the flag and superimposed upon it is an open Bible showing the beginning of St John's Gospel, 'In principio erat verbum', surmounted by a golden cross, symbolic of the Roman Catholic Church to which most of the people belong. The Bible is set upon four National Flags. The red symbolizes the blood and fire of revolutions; blue is for liberty; and the white cross stands for sacrifice in the cause of freedom. The motto, which means 'God, Fatherland and Liberty', was adopted as a slogan, which served also as a secret password, by Duarte.

ECUADOR. Republic of Ecuador (República del Ecuador).

The country came under Spanish rule in 1563 and was, at various times, subject to Peru and New Granada. After an abortive independence movement in 1809, it was liberated in 1822 and joined Bolivar's projected Greater Colombia; with the dissolution of the Union in 1830 it became a separate sovereign State. The formal declaration of independence was made on 10 August 1809. The Arms, which were introduced in 1845, display a snow-capped mountain (Chimborazo, the highest peak in the country) with an offshore steamer on the ocean in the foreground. In the sky above appear the sun accompanied by the four signs of the Zodiac appropriate to the months of March, April, May and June (relating to those months in the year 1845 when Ecuador was once again fighting for her liberty). Behind the oval on which the arms are depicted are four flags of the old Republic of Gran Colombia which, according to the designer, were intended to symbolize 'golden America separated by the blue sea from the bloodthirsty rule of Spain'. In Ecuador, however, which has based its own National Flag upon this, the gold is said to represent sunshine, grain and wealth; the blue, rivers, the ocean and the sky; the red being for the blood of the patriots who fought for freedom and justice. This idea of justice is better indicated by the fasces below the oval cartouche, which really symbolizes the republican institutions of the country. The South American location of the republic is indicated by the Andean condor.

EQUATORIAL GUINEA (Guinea Ecuatorial). Republic of Equatorial Guinea (República de Guinea Ecuatorial).

The former colony of Spanish Guinea comprised the islands of Fernando Po and Annobon, together with the mainland enclave of Rio Muni which itself included the offshore islands of Corisco, Elobey Grande and Elobey Chico; in all, six separate geographical entities. Fernando Po was discovered in the fifteenth century by the Portuguese and briefly settled by them in the seventeenth and eighteenth centuries, but was ceded to Spain in 1778. The British assumed administration in 1827 with the consent of Spain which, however, reclaimed the island in 1844. Rio Muni was awarded to Spain by the Treaty of Berlin in 1885. The whole territory was first represented in the Spanish Cortes in 1960 when the Africans were given equal status; in 1963 the colony was given self-government after a plebiscite and was renamed. In 1968 a further plebiscite led to complete independence which was proclaimed on 12 October. The new republic chose to indicate its unity by selecting as its State Coat-of-Arms the mangrove (or God Tree) while indicating its individual parts by means of the six stars above the shield. The motto means 'Unity, Peace, Justice'. The shield is sometimes gold and sometimes silver, and the mangrove tree recalls that the original treaty between Spain and King Bonkonto was signed under just such a tree.

ETHIOPIA (Ityopya). The Empire of Ethiopia (Ya Ytyopya Nigusa Nagast Manguist; or Mangesta Ityopya).

This is one of the very oldest countries of the world, but its history is almost impossible to summarize because of the way in which Ethiopia has been governed in the past. Nominally an empire under a single sovereign and a kingdom since ancient times, for a long time the real power lay in the hands of the dukes of the several regions into which it is divided. The country's history, therefore, has been influenced by a fight for continued freedom coupled with internal struggles for the Crown; indeed the country was finally brought to complete unity as recently as 1855 by the Emperor Theodore II who consolidated his conquest over Tigré and Shoa. The Emperor traces his ancestry to the Queen of Sheba and King Solomon and bears as his official title 'Conquering Lion of the Tribe of Judah, Elect of God, Emperor of Ethiopia'. The country is often claimed to be the oldest surviving Christian kingdom and certainly Christianity has existed there for many centuries, but it would appear to have been pagan until the fourth century A.D. when the Aksumite king was converted by Frumentius of Tyre; the Established Church (Coptic) adheres to Monophysitism. In view of the Emperor's august nomenclature it is not surprising that the Imperial Coat-of-Arms should be of the most imposing kind. It displays symbols of the Emperor's power, dignity and supremacy; upon the Throne of Solomon lies the orb. Before the throne, which is flanked by angels, one of which holds a sword and scales and the other a golden star, stands the Lion of Judah with a cross and streamers. Above the throne is the Bible in glory and at the foot is the Amharic legend 'The Conquering Lion of the Tribe of Judah'.

UNIDAD PAZ JUSTICIA

FIJI.

The Fijian Islands, which are no fewer than 322 in number, were discovered in 1643 by the Dutch navigator Tasman and were visited in 1774 by Captain James Cook. The first European settlement was established in 1804 and the missionaries began to arrive in 1835. Great Britain annexed the islands, after repeated requests by the tribal chiefs, and made them a Crown Colony in 1874. Full independence was achieved as a member of the British Commonwealth of Nations on 10 October 1970. The Coat-of-Arms, which was granted by Royal Warrant on 4 July 1908, was doubtless intended to be British in character, but the overall impression is of a distinctly English bias since it includes both the lion of England and the cross of St George. The shield also contains a representative selection of the island's produce in the form of sugar canes, a coconut palm, a bunch of bananas and a coconut. The crest is an outrigger canoe and the supporters are a pair of armed Fijians dressed in the characteristic *Tapa Sulu*, or mulberry-bark kilt. The motto may be translated 'Fear God, Honour the King'.

FINLAND (Suomi). Finnish Republic (Suomen Tasavalta; Republiken Finland).

The Finns, coming from the north and south-west, had by the eighth century A.D. taken most of the country from the Lapps, who receded northward. They in their turn were conquered in the twelfth century by the Swedes, whose King John III made the country a Grand Duchy in 1558. In 1721 Russia gained the province of Vyborg (Viipuri); additional areas were gained in 1743 and the remainder of the country was formally ceded to Russia in 1809. The country remained Russian until the revolution of 1917; independence was proclaimed on 6 December 1917 and this was recognized by the U.S.S.R. in 1920. The Arms were given by the Swedish king when the Grand Duchy was created; their earliest known appearance, however, is on the tomb of Gustaf Wasa in the cathedral of Uppsala. This provided the official pattern for the Arms when they were re-adopted after independence. They depict the Finnish Lion, brandishing a sword in its armoured paw, treading on a Russian scimitar (symbolizing the Russians, the Tartars and the peril from the East); the nine roses are today taken to represent the nine historical provinces of the country.

Rere · vaka · na · kalou · ka · doka · na · Tui

FRANCE. French Republic (République Française).
This State is unique in Europe in so far as its only official emblem is a flag. Although the French Royal House made use of the fleur-de-lys, which had been a royal emblem since the Dark Ages and thus formed one of the oldest emblems associated with any country, the revolution of 1789 inevitably swept it away; indeed, all heraldic display was proscribed.
With the successive French empires and monarchic restorations heraldry once again returned to favour, but in the republican interludes the State has never adopted Arms. It is true that a number of unofficial designs have been adopted, but it remains a fact that the official emblem as laid down in the Constitution is the tricolour; the emblem illustrated was adopted during the Third Republic as a quasi-official one and is still in semi-official use. The Roman fasces with axe and the motto 'Liberté, Égalité, Fraternité' (Liberty, Equality, Fraternity) effectively declare the republican nature of the device; to it are added, to increase its dignity, a sprig of olive and a sprig of oak, the whole being surrounded by the Collar of the Legion of Honour.

GABON. Gabonese Republic (République Gabonaise; *or* **République du Gabon).**
The country was called Gabão by the Portuguese sailors who visited the mouth of the Como River on the west coast of Africa because they thought the harbour resembled a certain kind of hooded coat which went by that name. Although this name was applied at first only to the harbour it was soon extended to the rest of the surrounding country. In 1885 the country was occupied by France and became a colony in 1888. Granted self-rule within the French Community in 1958, it secured complete independence on 17 August 1960. The State Coat-of-Arms which was adopted in 1963 represents the country and makes use of the colours of the National Flag; green represents the great dense forests; yellow, the sun; blue, the sea; and black, the people of Africa. The three gold discs indicate the mineral resources of Gabon; the ship stands for the progressive will of the nation and indicates the importance of the sea. Behind the shield appears the trunk of the Okume tree (*Aucoumea klaineana*) which is of economic importance. The inscription above means 'United we shall go forward', that at the foot means 'Unity, Work, Justice'.

THE GAMBIA. The Republic of the Gambia.

Until the fifteenth century this country was part of the African empires of Ghana and Songhai and was unknown to Europeans. With the arrival of the Portuguese in 1455 the Gambia River was explored and settlements were established on its banks; the British arrived in 1588 and made it a colony in 1821. The Gambia was granted independence within the Commonwealth on 18 February 1965 and became a republic in April 1970. The Arms, which were granted by Royal Warrant on 18 November 1964, show a Locar axe and a Mandinka hoe in the shield and also held in the paws of the lion supporters. The crest is an oil palm nut tree, which is indigenous to the country and represents natural resources.

GERMANY (Deutschland). German Democratic Republic (Deutsche Demokratische Republik).

This state was established by the Constitution of 7 October 1949 enacted by a provisional People's Chamber. Its legality is not accepted by any of the Western countries and it was most certainly established as an answer to its Western counterpart; it was acknowledged as a Sovereign State by the U.S.S.R. in 1955. The State Emblem was introduced in the latter year and deviates strongly from the normal heraldic coat-of-arms associated with Western Europe; it has been designed according to the Soviet pattern and so shows a pronounced Communist influence. It consists of a hammer (representing the workers and industry) and a pair of compasses (representing science and technology) set within a wreath of grain (representing farms and agriculture). The ribbon follows the pattern of the flag.

PROGRESS PEACE PROSPERITY

GERMANY (Deutschland). Federal Republic of Germany (Bundesrepublik Deutschland).
For most of its history Germany has been divided into a large number of separate states
which have, at times, been loosely grouped together in such institutions as the Holy Roman
Empire and the Zollverein. In 1848 an attempt was made by a group of revolutionaries
(including Marx and Engels) to overthrow the government and set up a republic; their aim
was to unite all Germany into one nation. They were not successful, but unity was achieved
in 1870 when the Second Empire was proclaimed; even this included kingdoms, grand
duchies and so on. This lasted until 1918 when the country became a republic. With the
defeat of the Nazi regime the country was divided into the Allied Zones of occupation, and
by 1946 these had hardened almost into two separate States. The Federal Republic came
into existence on 23 May 1949 and attained full sovereignty in 1955. It was formed from
the former French, British and American zones both of Germany as a whole and of the
city of Berlin. In 1950 the republic readopted as its Arms the black eagle which had so long
represented Germany. It can be traced back to about A.D. 1100, but ultimately derives
from the Roman eagle. At first the eagle had only one head, but later that of the emperor
came to have two, the single-headed variety being regarded as the prerogative of the
German king. For over a thousand years the eagle has had German associations and in 1919
the republic adopted it as its Arms.

GHANA. The Republic of Ghana.
This country takes its name from a former State with which it has no connection whatever.
When Europe was a collection of tiny backward countries, there was in western Africa a
great kingdom; this was called Ghana and it lasted for some six hundred years. In 1077 the
people were defeated by a Moslem army, but the kingdom's final destruction did not destroy
the memory of it. The modern Ghana was settled by the Portuguese in 1482; after their
withdrawal the dominant powers were Britain and the Netherlands. The latter's withdrawal
in 1872 left the field clear for the British, and in 1872 the Crown Colony of the Gold Coast
was set up; to this was added in 1900 (by annexation) Ashanti and, in 1922 (as a mandate)
part of Togoland. The country obtained full internal self-government in 1954 and ultimate
complete independence as a member of the British Commonwealth on 6 March 1957; in
1960 it became a republic. The State Coat-of-Arms was granted by Royal Warrant on 4
March 1957 and includes the British (really English) lion on a cross; surrounding the cross
are a linguist's stick (an emblem of authority) and a ceremonial sword (for the
administration), a castle (for the national government), a cocoa tree and a gold mine (for
the main produce and activities). The star is the guiding star of African freedom.

FREEDOM JUSTICE AND

GREECE (Ellas). Kingdom of the Hellenes (Vasileion tis Ellados).
After the country had been under a succession of foreign powers since 146 B.C., and since A.D. 1453 a part of the Ottoman Empire, Greek dreams of independence were stimulated in the early nineteenth century and in 1821 there began the final War of Independence. Turkey recognized Greek autonomy in 1829 and the European powers recognized its complete independence in 1832. The first sovereign was Otto I, a Bavarian prince whose rule proved to be authoritarian and unpopular; in 1862 he was deposed and a Danish prince was elected to the throne as King George I. The National Coat-of-Arms (the white cross on blue) was adopted in 1832 and shows the colours of the Royal House of Bavaria; they are supposed to represent the Christian faith. The Royal Arms are formed by placing upon this shield the Danish Royal Arms as borne by King Christian IX; the supporters are two figures of Hercules. In their present form these Arms date from 1863, and the shield is surrounded by the Cordon of the Order of the Redeemer. The motto, which is the Greek translation of Christian IX's parting words to his son Prince William (George I) means 'The love of the people is my strength'.

GUATEMALA. Republic of Guatemala (República de Guatemala).
The Spanish Captaincy-General of Guatemala was set up in 1524 and lasted until 1821; in that year the country became independent of Spain but was annexed to the Mexican Empire. Regaining its independence, it became the nucleus of the United Provinces of Central America (usually known as the Central American Federation); this broke up in 1838–9 as one State after another seceded; each went its own way, but none of them ever quite forgot the Federation. Guatemala became a republic in 1847 and had already adopted a State Emblem somewhat similar to the present one by 1843. The present design dates from 1871 and shows the quetzal bird (*Paramocrus mocinno*); this is the national bird of the country, deriving from a local Indian legend as the 'bird of freedom', and is here intended as a symbol of liberty. It is perched upon a scroll inscribed with the date of independence from Spain set in front of rifles and sabres (symbolizing the readiness of the people to defend their freedom). The whole is enclosed by a wreath of laurel tied with a ribbon of the national colours, blue (representing the desire for perfection) and white (representing the hope for peace).

50

GUINEA (Guinée). Republic of Guinea (République de Guinée).

From the sixteenth century until the nineteenth century Guinea was the happy hunting ground of slave traders. After a series of wars and agreements with tribal chiefs, the country was annexed by France under the name Rivières du Sud. In 1893 it was renamed French Guinea and in 1895 became part of French West Africa; it remained an overseas French territory until it was proclaimed an independent republic on 2 October 1958. The State Coat-of-Arms declares that the country is African and that it avows a neutral course in international affairs. The significance of the colours may be the same as in the flag, in which red stands for the blood shed in the struggle for freedom, yellow for the sunshine and gold, and green for the trees and plants. These three colours have come to be known as the 'Pan-African colours' and have been generally adopted as the symbol of African unity; as such they appear in the flags of Senegal, Mali, Guinea, Ghana, Togo, Dahomey, Cameroun, Congo-Brazzaville and Rwanda. They are also the colours of Ethiopia, the oldest independent State in Africa, which adopted them in 1894. The motto means 'Work, Justice, Solidarity'.

GUYANA. The Co-operative Republic of Guyana.

The first European settlement in this country was made by the Dutch in 1581, and for two centuries the French, Portuguese and British vied with one another to replace the settlements. Out of the tug-of-war which ensued there emerged a British, French and Dutch colony. The colony of British Guiana was established in 1814 and its name was taken from an Amerindian word meaning 'Land of Waters'. The country was granted independence on 26 May 1966, having previously been granted internal self-government in 1961, and the name was changed. On 23 February 1970 it became a republic though remaining within the British Commonwealth. The State Coat-of-Arms was granted on 21 January 1966 and includes a conventional representation of water (in allusion to the name) between a giant waterlily (*Victoria regia*) showing one leaf and two flowers, one open and the other opening, and in the base a Canje pheasant. The crest is a Cacique's (i.e. an Indian chieftain) crown between two diamonds; the supporters are two jaguars holding a miner's pick and a sugar cane, emblematic of the country and its main products.

TRAVAIL JUSTICE SOLIDARITE

ONE PEOPLE ONE NATION ONE DESTINY

HAITI. Republic of Haiti (République d'Haïti).

This country shares the Caribbean island of Hispaniola with the Dominican Republic. After its discovery by Columbus the region now known as Haiti was ignored by the Spanish and consequently the influence of other nations began to be felt. French colonists began the development of sugar plantations in the north; in 1677 the French seized the land and made it a colony; in 1697 Spain was finally obliged to cede Haiti to France. Haiti proclaimed itself an independent republic in 1804 and for a number of years the country was in chaos, experiencing various forms of government including a Negro Empire. The State Emblem was designed in 1807 by the then President, Alexander Sabès Petion. It displays a palm tree on a green mount accompanied by all the panoply of war; until 1963 the tree was surmounted by a pole bearing the cap of liberty. The flags are black (for the people of pure African descent) and red (for the mulattos, or those of mixed African and European descent). The motto means 'Unity gives strength'.

HONDURAS. Republic of Honduras (República de Honduras).

In company with the rest of the Central American States, Honduras became independent on 15 September 1821. It entered the Mexican Empire, but in 1825 joined the Central American Federation of which a Honduran, Francisco Morazán, was President. Honduras became an independent republic on 5 November 1838 and the State Emblem has been in use since that time. The triangle in the emblem is taken from the emblem of the United Provinces and symbolizes equality and justice, the water around it representing the Pacific and Atlantic Oceans. The two towers represent sovereignty and independence. The cornucopias symbolize the natural resources of the country whilst the trees and tools indicate the extent to which trees and their products—timber, bananas, coffee, etc.—figure in the economy. The inscription around the oval means 'Republic of Honduras, Free, Sovereign, Independent, 15 September 1821'.

L'UNION FAIT LA FORCE

REPᶜᵃ DE HONDURAS LIBRE SOBERANA INDEPENDIENTE
15 SEPTᴮᴿᴱ 1821

HUNGARY (Magyarország). Hungarian People's Republic (Magyar Népköztársaság).
Hungary was formed in 1918 out of the ruins of Austro-Hungary. In 1949 the old
Hungarian Arms, which are known from about 1200, were replaced by a State Emblem of
the conventional Soviet pattern. The present State Emblem was introduced after the 1956
revolution; it is more neutral in pattern than the former one and consists of a gold-edged
shield of the national colours set upon a pale-blue field upon which are golden beams
radiating from the red Communist star above. The customary wreath of grain is here
entwined with two different ribbons, one in the national colours and one red, which are
tied together in a bow; this is a most unusual arrangement.

ICELAND (Island). Republic of Iceland (Lýdhveldidh Island).
Iceland was settled by Norsemen in the ninth century A.D. and in the thirteenth century
Norwegian suzerainty was acknowledged; in 1380 it passed, with Norway, to the Danish
Crown, and a national decline set in. The nineteenth century saw a rebirth of national
culture bringing in its wake agitation for independence. This was attained gradually; in
1874 limited home rule was granted, in 1918 Iceland was declared an independent kingdom
in union with the Crown of Denmark. The German occupation of the latter country proved
to be a decisive factor in the search for independence, and on 17 June 1944 an independent
republic was proclaimed. The National Coat-of-Arms of Iceland is identical with the
Icelandic flag, which recalls the flag of Norway, the order of the colours being reversed;
adopted in 1919, when it included the Royal Crown as a kingdom, it continues in use as
the Arms of the republic. The whole achievement is unusual in that it has no fewer than
four supporters; these are a dragon, a vulture, a bull and a giant, taken from Snorre
Storlason's *Heimskringla*, representing the guardian spirits of the land, set upon what is
presumably a representation of a rocky coastline.

INDIA (Bharat). The Indian Union (*or* Republic of India) (Bharat Juktarashtra; *or* Bharat ka Ganatranta).

Never in its history has the whole Indian subcontinent been united under a single State. Even in the days of the British Raj the presence of French and Portuguese enclaves marred the prospect of unity, and at the present time, when these enclaves have been eliminated, the republics of India and Pakistan reflect a sometimes hostile division. Leaving aside the history of the numerous states which constituted the Indian Empire, it is apparent that one of the greatest rulers was the emperor Asoka (died 232 B.C.), who for the first time brought nearly all India under one sway. It is little wonder then that the republic of India, which gained independence on 15 July 1947 and became a republic on 26 January 1950, chose as its State Emblem (in 1950) the capital of the Asoka pillar at Sarnath. This was erected to commemorate the place where the Buddha first proclaimed his gospel; the symbolism of the device is too complex to be discussed here, but it might be pointed out that the item of greatest significance is not the lions, which may have originally supported the solar disc, but the 'Wheel of the Law'. The emblem has no specific colour, but when appearing alone it is often yellow.

INDONESIA. Republic of Indonesia (Republik Indonesia).

The territories now forming Indonesia became subject to the Dutch Government in 1799 and, with a brief interval of British rule between 1811 and 1815, under that rule they remained until 28 December 1949 when the Union of Indonesia was proclaimed. The United States of Indonesia, as it then became, was loosely linked with the Netherlands under the Dutch Crown, but even this loose union was dissolved on 10 August 1954. The State Coat-of-Arms was adopted in 1950 for the unitary state of the Indonesian Republic and is borne on the breast of the legendary Garuda Bird; this mythological creature will be discussed with reference to Thailand. The shield displays an ox's head (symbolizing the people's struggle for independence), a *waringin* tree (representing the vitality of the nation), a branch of the cotton tree and a sprig of rice (for the welfare of the people), and a chain (symbolizing their faith in the equality of all men and the unification of all islands and races in Indonesia). The unity of the nation is further represented by the centre shield placed over a narrow black horizontal band to indicate that Indonesia lies on the Equator. The motto means 'Unity through diversity'.

BHINNEKA TUNGGAL IKA

IRAN. Empire of Iran (Keshvaré Shahanshahiyé Irân).

Persia, as Iran was formerly known to Europeans, is one of those nations that have existed for such a long time that their origins are lost in remote antiquity. It is not known precisely when the Persian Empire was founded by Cyrus the Great (who died in 529 B.C.), but October 1971 officially marked the 2,500th anniversary of the founding of the monarchy. The Pahlavi dynasty which at present occupies the throne came to power by a *coup d'état* in 1921; the position then was a military dictatorship, but in 1925 Reza Khan was elected hereditary Shah. The Imperial State Emblem is of unknown total significance but something is known of the component parts. The lion and sun have been in use since the Middle Ages and appear to have had, originally, both royal and religious significance. The Pahlavi Crown and the sword were both added in 1842.

IRAQ (Iraq). The Democratic People's Republic of Iraq (Al Djumhuriet al-Iraqîyah al democratîyah aschabîyah).

Iraq became a British mandate in 1920, being raised to the dignity of a kingdom in the following year. When the mandate came to an end in 1932 the country became independent. In 1958 the merger of Syria and Egypt to form the United Arab Republic led the rulers of the neighbouring kingdoms of Iraq and Jordan to announce the federation of their States as the Arab Union. This was rapidly dissolved, however, for the Army seized Baghdad and the royal family of Iraq was murdered. The Republic of Iraq was proclaimed 14 July 1958 and took its present title upon a change in the constitution in 1969. The Arms were introduced in 1965 and, although the legend on the plaque may have changed in accordance with the constitutional alteration, they are still in use. A shield derived from the National Flag is placed upon the breast of the Saladin eagle which holds a plaque of the country's name. This arrangement is becoming almost as typical of an Arab country as is the wreath of grain typical of a Communist one.

الجمهورية العراقية

IRELAND (Éire). Republic of Ireland (Poblacht na hÉireann).

Some Irish historians have traced the succession of the native kings to about the period of the Flood 'before which time were many princes'. The records, needless to say, have not been preserved and such history rests upon tradition. However, much can be learned about the troubled state of the country from the traditional lists of monarchs. Of the 169 rulers alleged to have ruled between 1285 B.C. and the Christian Era, only fifteen died comfortably in their beds, four dying of the plague or some malignant disease, the rest being either assassinated, killed in battle or dying other violent deaths. Home Rule was in existence from the earliest times, but on the basis of petty tribal kingdoms united loosely under the paramount head of the *Ard Righ*. The country was conquered by Henry II of England in 1272 and was declared to be a kingdom during the reign of Henry VIII, being formally united within the United Kingdom in 1801. The whole country, with the exception of six of the northern counties, became independent once more in 1922 with the establishment of the Irish Free State as a British Dominion. A Republic of Ireland was proclaimed in 1948 and was recognized by Great Britain in the following year. The Arms of the Republic consist of those assigned to the kingdom during the reign of Henry VIII, also being retained as a part of those of the United Kingdom. The first Arms borne after independence combined the arms of the four provinces composing the Republic.

ISRAEL (Yisrael). State of Israel (Medinat Yisrael).

The first steps towards the establishment of a Jewish national state may be said to have been taken in 1917 when the British Government, in the Balfour Declaration, declared itself in favour of a home for the Jews. The following year saw Palestine pass under British rule as a League of Nations mandate and Jews began to enter the country. Naturally this caused resentment on the part of the Arabs who had for so long occupied the country and the following years saw much disturbance. The 1947 United Nations plan for partition of the country failed, but in 1949 a State of Israel was recognized by the West; subsequent history is too well known to require repetition here. For centuries the Menorah, the seven-branched candlestick which had adorned the Temple, has been regarded as a pre-eminently Jewish symbol and is indeed found, as such, in the Roman catacombs. It was officially proclaimed to be the official emblem of the State on 10 February 1949. To it are added two olive branches and the word Israel in Hebrew.

62

ITALY (Italia). Italian Republic (Repùbblica Italiana).
This country has known, in the course of history, virtually every form of government which
the imagination of man is able to conceive. After the fall of the Western Roman Empire
the country dissolved by a gradual process into a conglomeration of diminutive states
embracing a wide range of types. The process of reunification was a long and arduous one,
the complete unity of the country being finally achieved only in 1870 under the King of
Sardinia when Rome once more became the capital city. The Republic of San Marino alone
retained its independent form of government, although entirely enclosed by the Italian
dominions; the precise position of the Vatican at that time would be difficult to determine.
After the Second World War, during which a complex form of government known as a
Fascist 'synodical-corporative' state was set up, there was considerable dissatisfaction with
the monarchy and the referendum of 2 June 1946 declared in favour of a republic by a small
majority. The new Constitution was approved 22 December 1947, and Article 1 declares
Italy to be 'a Democratic Republic founded upon work'. This is reflected in the State
Emblem which combines the Socialist star with a cogwheel. The whole has a decidedly
Communist flavour.

IVORY COAST (Côte d'Ivoire). Republic of Ivory Coast (République de Côte d'Ivoire).
In pre-colonial times the country was dominated by African kingdoms among which the
Portuguese established trading settlements in the sixteenth century. A flourishing trade in
ivory and slaves quickly developed. In 1842 the first French settlement was established; in
that same year a French protectorate was imposed over the coastal zone and extended to
the entire country in 1893, when it became a French colony. Agitation for independence
was intensified by the Second World War, and this was rewarded in 1956 by a grant of
internal autonomy within the French Community. The country, however, soon withdrew,
and on 7 August 1960 it became a sovereign independent republic. The Arms were adopted
upon full independence and bear an elephant's head, with the tusks from which the country
derives its name. The flanking palm trees indicate natural resources, palm-oil being one of
the country's main products.

JAMAICA. Territory of Jamaica.

The island was discovered by Christopher Columbus in 1494 and it remained under Spanish rule until 1655 when the British captured it. Spain formally ceded the island to Britain in 1670. At first it prospered from the wealth brought by the buccaneers, notable among whom was Sir Henry Morgan, to the capital Port Royal; but the town was destroyed by earthquake in 1692. Following the destruction of the Arawak Indians by the Spanish a new population of Negro slaves had been introduced. Slavery was abolished in 1833, but the over-population of the island, coupled with economic decline, generated tension and unrest. In 1944 the island was granted internal self-government, but it was not until the next decade that the rapid changes which led to nationhood were brought about. Jamaica became a fully independent member of the British Commonwealth of Nations on 6 August 1962, thus ending a period of 307 years of British rule. The Arms, which had appeared on the colony's seal granted by Royal Warrant on 3 February 1661, are supposed to have been designed by William Sandcroft, a seventeenth-century Archbishop of Canterbury. Until 8 April 1957, however, there had never been a definitive grant of them, and the motto was changed on 13 July 1962. They include the characteristic pineapples, which are one of the most important products of the island, and are supported by two Arawak Indians.

JAPAN (Nippon). Empire of Japan (Nippon-Koku).

Japan, like Iran (*q.v.*), is a country whose origins are lost in the mists of antiquity. The rulers have claimed descent from the sun-goddess and, until 1945, it was held as dogma that the empire was a divine design and was founded in 660 B.C. by the Emperor Jimmu. Actually reliable records date back only to about A.D. 400. With the rise to power of the Shoguns (military dictators) the emperors became mere puppet figure-heads, and few people in the West were even aware of their existence until well into the nineteenth century. The westernization of the country began in 1859 after the conclusion of a treaty between Japan and the U.S.A. The last Shogun abdicated in 1868 and the emperor resumed effective rule. Since that time the country has become increasingly westernized, and after the Second World War almost completely so. The principle of imperial divinity has been abandoned, and this is reflected in what is now regarded as the State Emblem. There has never been any system of 'heraldry' in Japan, but there is a system which closely resembles it; this consists of badges, known as *Mon*. That of the State is really the Imperial Mon (but not that personal to the emperor) and consists of a stylized chrysanthemum flower of sixteen petals, which is called *Ki-ku-non-hana-mon* (the most distinguished device of the Imperial House).

OUT OF MANY, ONE PEOPLE

JORDAN (Al-'Urdun). The Hashemite Kingdom of Jordan (Al Mamlaka al-'Urdunnîyah al Haschimîyah).

The land now forming the kingdom was overrun by the Moslem Turks in the mid seventh century and remained under the rule of the various caliphates, with the exception of a brief period under the Latin kingdom of Jerusalem, until its fall to the Ottoman Empire. It remained under Turkish rule until the end of the First World War. In 1920 it became part of the short-lived kingdom of Syria, but was quickly brought to heel by the British by whom it was administered as part of the Palestine mandate. In 1923 Great Britain agreed to recognize its independence, but this did not come about, for in that year, despite some opposition from Zionist groups, an administrative agreement made Britain suzerain. The country's loyalty during the Second World War led to the termination of the mandate and the proclamation of the kingdom as an independent state on 25 May 1946 (the country had become independent on 22 March). In 1958 Jordan and Iraq formed the short-lived Arab Union, which came to an end because of the Iraqi revolution. The State Arms date from 1921, and the eagle has subsequently become the favourite emblem in those countries which subscribe to the Pan-Arab concept. It stands upon a blue globe, symbolizing the spread of Islam throughout the world, and appears in conjunction with weapons (for Islamic conquests), ears of wheat and palm branch (for agriculture), and the Badge of the 1st Class of the Order of the Resurrection. The scroll bears the inscription 'Al-Hussein Ibn Talal Ibn Abdullah, King of the Hashemite Kingdom of Jordan, who prays that God may bring him happiness and help'.

KENYA. Republic of Kenya (Djumhuri ya Kenya).

The coastal area of Kenya was settled in the seventh century by Arabs trading in ivory and slaves, and by the time the Portuguese arrived in 1498 Indians and Chinese were also living there. The Oman Arabs defeated the Portuguese in 1729 and regained control, and in 1886 the British received a concession of the coastal strip from the Sultan of Zanzibar. The financial difficulties of the British East Africa Company led Britain to declare a protectorate over Kenya in 1895; in 1920 the protectorate (with the exception of the coastal strip) became a Crown Colony. Preparations for independence began in 1954, and full independence was achieved 12 December 1963. The country became a republic on 12 December 1964. The Arms, which were granted by Royal Warrant 12 December 1963, are borne on an African warrior's shield; the colours refer to the people, the struggle for independence and the country's agriculture. The cockerel holds aloft an axe—this is said, according to tribal customs, to herald a new prosperous life—and the shield is supported by two lions grasping spears of state standing upon a compartment which represents Mount Kenya, upon which grow the principal products of the country (coffee, camomile, sisal, tea, maize and pineapple). The Swahili motto means 'Together' (i.e. Let us work together).

KOREA (Choson *or* Han Guk). Korean People's Democratic Republic (Choson Minchu-Chui Imnin Konghwa-Guk).

Korea was made a vassal-state of Manchu China in the early seventeenth century and became isolated from all foreign contact, all non-Chinese influences being rigorously excluded until 1876 when Japan forced a commercial treaty with Korea. Soon the U.S.A. and other countries were admitted to her trade, and in 1910 the country passed under Japanese control, under which it remained until the Japanese capitulation at the end of the Second World War. Korea was then arbitrarily divided into two zones of occupation, with the 38th parallel of latitude as the line of demarcation, this division being formalized in 1948 when the two separate regimes were established. The People's Republic (better known as North Korea) was founded 1 May 1948 and its State Emblem dates from that time. It depicts a hydro-electric power station surrounded by a wreath of rice and is surmounted by the usual five-pointed red star. The scroll at the base is inscribed with the name of the country.

KOREA (Choson *or* Han Guk). Republic of Korea (Dae Han Min Guk).

This republic was formally proclaimed 15 August 1948, and since that time has been in almost continuous conflict with its northern neighbour. Its State Emblem, unlike that of the North, recalls the past not the future; it is based upon that of the old kingdom of Korea which came to an end in 1910. Its symbolism is practically inexhaustible, especially when taken in conjunction with those devices which appear on the National Flag; the Yin-Yang represents many things, but principally it symbolizes that there are two sides to everything— good and evil, night and day, male and female, etc. It may possibly represent two fishes placed side by side and head to tail, but the whole thing signifies the reconciliation of opposing tendencies in nature.

KUWAIT (Al Kuwait). State of Kuwait (Dowlat al Kuwait).

This small Moslem state, which owes its immense wealth to its rich oil fields, derives from the settlements established some three hundred years ago on the shore at the head of the Persian Gulf by people from Central Arabia. They became fishermen, shipbuilders and merchants. The British began to direct the State's foreign affairs in 1899 and the country resumed full independence only on 19 June 1961. Bearing in mind the country's origins, the Emblem of the Emir displays an Arab dhow on the sea within the encircling wings of a falcon bearing a shield as the National Flag; the inscription at the top is the name of the country. The colours of the shield and flag are the traditional Moslem ones, but in Kuwait these are held to have special symbolism. Thus red symbolizes traditional horsemanship and bravery in war; white the country's great achievements; and green the wish for growing things. An alternative symbolism reads 'White is our deeds, black our battlefields, green our pastures, and red, dyed with the blood of the enemy, is our future'.

LAOS. Kingdom of Laos (Praha Raja Ananchak Lao; Royaume de Laos).

This kingdom was founded in the thirteenth century and was once known by the name of Lanzang (The Land of a Million Elephants). Internal dissension brought about division and, after France had begun exploration of the interior in the late nineteenth century, a French protectorate was established in 1893. In spite of strong nationalist sentiments, France re-established dominion over the whole country and made the King of Luang Prabang the constitutional monarch over the whole country. On 19 July 1949 it became a semi-autonomous state within the French Union, and by 1954 had achieved full independence. It formally left the French Union on 7 December 1956. The State Emblem includes three elephants to symbolize the unification of three principalities under one dynasty. The white parasols are symbols of monarchy, whilst the steps symbolize the commandments of Buddhism.

72

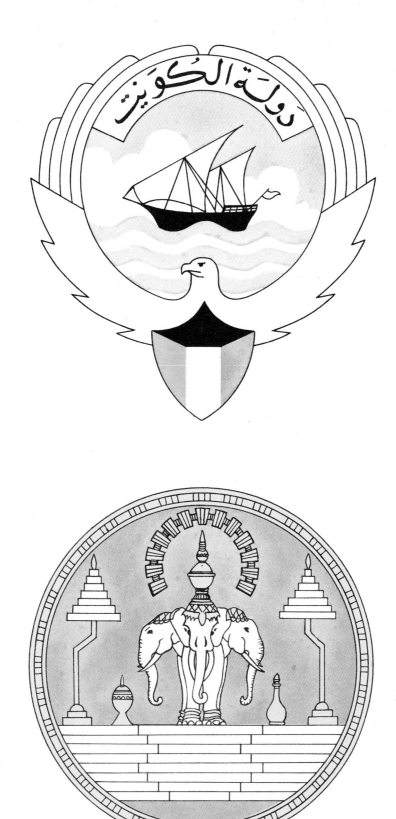

LEBANON (Lubnan). Republic of Lebanon (Al Jumhuriyah al Lubnaniyah).
This country has a long history; Hittites, Aramaeans, Phoenicians, Assyrians, Persians, Greeks, Romans, Byzantines, Arabs, Crusaders and Turks, all have played their part up to the time when European influence became predominant. After the First World War Lebanon passed under French mandate in company with Syria; this caused much discontent and there was a strong desire for independence. By treaty, in 1936, France provided for independence after a transition period of three years; unfortunately these provisions were not ratified before war once more broke out. The coastal area of the country was captured by the British and Free French from the Vichy régime in mid 1941 and Lebanon was proclaimed an independent republic, but this did not become an accomplished fact until 1 January 1944. For its State Emblem the republic chose one entirely representative of the country; while under the French mandate its flag bore a 'cedar of Lebanon' and this was made the central feature of the new Arms. It symbolizes strength, holiness and immortality; the red is for self-sacrifice and the white for peace.

LESOTHO. Kingdom of Lesotho.
The early Bushman inhabitants of this region were supplanted at the beginning of the nineteenth century by the Bechuana, and the present inhabitants represent the remnants of several tribes broken up by the Zulu and Matabele. As a country its history is comparatively short, since these scattered tribes were rallied only in 1820 by Moshoshoe, a paramount chief, who established a dynasty here. In 1868 the British established a protectorate over the country and gave it the name of Basutoland. Independence was once more attained on 4 October 1966. The Arms are representative of the country and are borne upon a Lesotho battle shield. The Arms consist of a crocodile, the badge of the former Basutoland and the Lesotho national beast. Behind the shield, which is supported by horses, appear ostrich feathers, an assegai and a knobkerrie. The compartment, in the form of the summit of the Thaba Bosiu Mountain, bears the motto 'Peace, Rain, Abundance'.

KHOTSO PULA NALA

LIBERIA. Republic of Liberia.

This country owes its foundation to the enterprise of certain American citizens; in 1822 agents of the American Colonization Society purchased an area on the coast, near the present Monrovia, for the settlement of freed slaves from the United States. The descendants of these settlers have provided the governing group of Liberia, which was proclaimed a republic 26 July 1847. For its continued existence it has owed much to the United States, upon whose constitution and government its own is closely based. The State Arms depict a landscape with a plough in front of a seashore upon which grows a palm tree. This represents the tools with which the freed slaves cultivated their new land. In the background is the ship which brought them to Africa and overhead flies a dove carrying the Declaration of Independence with the setting sun in the background. The motto declares the country's origins, a feature which is heightened by the occasional appearance of the National Flags crossed behind the shield. In this the eleven stripes recall the signatories of the Declaration of Liberian Independence, the blue field represents the African continent, and the star represents the republic. It is not difficult to see the close resemblance between the National Flags of Liberia and the U.S.A.

LIBYA (Al Libiyya). Libyan Arab Republic (Al Djumhurîyet al-Arabîye al-Libiyya).

For more than two thousand years this country has been claimed by a succession of invaders. In ancient times it was successively under the Carthaginians, the Romans and the Vandals; in the Middle Ages Egypt and Tunisia contended for control, and for a time in the early sixteenth century Spain and the Knights of Malta held dominion. In 1551 the Ottoman Empire took Libya and Moslem influence became paramount. After the Turco-Italian War (1911–12) Italy proclaimed its annexation, but was forced to embark upon a long series of wars of pacification before it could attain that end. After the Allied victory over the Axis powers in North Africa in 1943 Libya was placed first of all under an Anglo-French military government and later under the administration of the United Nations; the population demanded independence. Preparations for this were begun on United Nations recommendation after the Allied powers had failed to agree about the country's future, and the united Kingdom of Libya became formally independent on 24 December 1951. On 1 September 1969, however, the king was deposed in his absence by a group of army officers who formed a Revolutionary Command Council and declared the country a republic. The State Coat-of-Arms introduced in 1969 is based upon that of the United Arab Republic (see Arab Republic of Egypt) with the appropriate changes in the shield and inscription, thus showing the influence of the Pan-Arab concept.

LIECHTENSTEIN. Principality of Liechtenstein (Fürstentum Liechtenstein).

This small principality, which has an area of only sixty-two square miles, came into existence on 23 June 1719 when it was created as an immediate fief of the Holy Roman Empire by the Emperor Charles VI. The county of Vaduz and the barony of Schellenburg were then united under the name of the family which had purchased them; the princes rarely visited their country, but were active in the service of the Habsburg monarchy. The principality did not achieve sovereign independence (and then only a nominal one) until 1806 upon the fall of the empire, and on 12 July 1806 it took its place as a member of the Confederation of the Rhine. Total independence ultimately came in 1918, although it had remained neutral during the First World War and had not followed Austria, with which it had a customs union. The Princely Arms are truly dynastic and include quarterings for Silesia, Kuenringe, the duchy of Troppau, the counties of Ostfriesland and Rietberg, and the duchy of Jägerndorf; overall on a small shield are the patronomial arms of the ruling House of Liechtenstein. The crown is that appropriate to a prince of the Holy Roman Empire.

LUXEMBOURG. The Grand Duchy of Luxembourg (Grand-Duché de Luxembourg; Grousherzogdem Letzeburg; Grossherzogtum Luxemburg).

The county of Luxembourg goes back to the tenth century; in A.D. 963 a French prince built a fortress called Lucilinburhuc on a rocky hill amid the lands he controlled. Later called Lützelburg, it became the centre of the modern state. It was one of the largest fiefs in the Holy Roman Empire and rose to prominence when its ruler was elected emperor as Henry VII in 1308; his grandson the emperor Charles IV raised it to the dignity of a duchy in 1354. In 1443 Philip the Good of Burgundy seized the duchy and was confirmed in possession by the Estates in 1451; in 1482 it passed to the House of Habsburg and thenceforward shared the history of the South Netherlands. The Congress of Vienna made it a grand duchy in union with the newly founded kingdom of the Netherlands and at the same time it became a member of the German Confederation. With the Belgian revolt in 1830 part of the grand duchy passed to that kingdom; the remaining portion became autonomous and was granted a constitution in 1848. Nevertheless the union with the crown of the Netherlands continued and was finally severed in 1890 on the death of William III. The Arms have been in existence since the beginning of the thirteenth century and several different versions appear at the present time according to the purpose for which they are used. The shield is surrounded by the Grand Cordon of the Order of the Oaken Crown.

MADAGASCAR. Malagasy Republic (Repoblika Malagasy; République Malgache).
The original inhabitants of this island probably came from south-east Asia (perhaps
Indonesia) via South India in early times; somewhat later a dark-skinned people moved on
to the island from Africa. Malagasy history tells us that Arab colonies were established
from the ninth to the fourteenth centuries; by the sixteenth century native kingdoms were
flourishing. In 1500 the Portuguese discovered Mogadisho which was misnamed Madagascar;
they, the English and the French vainly attempted to found permanent settlements and the
island became the haunt of pirates. King Radama I (1810–28) established friendly relations
with the British; after 1810 the British and French began to compete with each other for
control of the island, and by 1855 the latter had won. They established a protectorate in
1885 and ruled the island until 1960. Increased self-government was granted in 1956, and in
1958 the island voted to become the Malagasy Republic within the French Union, an
autonomous state associated with France. The Malagasy Republic achieved full independence
on 20 June 1960, but elected to remain in the French Community. The State Emblem
appeared in 1959 and consists of an ox-head between rice plants and a ranivala palm; the
State Seal also bears the republic's title.

MALAWI. Republic of Malawi.
Nyasaland, as this country was formerly called, was first visited by Portuguese explorers in
the seventeenth and eighteenth centuries, and was rediscovered in 1859 by the explorer-
missionary David Livingstone, who made a journey inland from the east coast of Africa to
Lake Nyasa. The country was already well known to Arab slave-traders whom the British
undertook to subdue; the British also defeated in 1889 the Portuguese attempt to annex the
southern uplands to Mozambique. A British protectorate of British Central Africa was set
up in 1891; despite determined opposition from the Africans Nyasaland was joined in 1953
to the Federation of Rhodesia and Nyasaland. As a result of elections held in 1961 the
Africans gained control of the legislative council, and in November 1962 Britain and
Nyasaland agreed to self-government within the Federation. On 6 July 1966 the country
became independent within the Commonwealth and also became a republic on that day. The
State Coat-of-Arms was granted by Royal Warrant on 30 June 1964 and reflects the principal
features of the country; the sun in the base is taken from the former Arms of Nyasaland,
the wavy 'chief' representing the lakes of the country. The lion and the leopard are
indigenous to Malawi, as is the fish-eagle in the crest. The shield stands on a compartment
representing the Mlanje Mountain.

UNITY AND FREEDOM

MALAYSIA. Federation of Malaysia (Persekutuan Tanah Melaysiu).
The State Coat-of-Arms of the Federation sets out in heraldic detail the State's composition and is a commentary upon its history. The present design dates from 1967 and is the latest step in the development of a coat which was approved by Her Majesty Queen Elizabeth II on 18 March 1952. The four plain coloured quarters in the centre represent the States of Selangor, Pahang, Perak and Negri Sembilan, which were formed into the Federated Malay States in 1895; the five daggers (or *kris*) represent the States of Johore, Kedah, Perlis, Kelantan and Trengganu (the unfederated States) which joined the other four in 1948 to form the Federation of Malaya. The two outer divisions contain the Arms of Penang and Malacca which formed part of the Federation in 1948; in the base were added in 1963 quarterings for Sabah (formerly British North Borneo), Singapore and Sarawak. Singapore seceded in 1965 and its place in the shield was taken in 1967 by the national flower of Malaysia, *Hibiscus rosa-sinensis*. Above the shield is the Crescent of Islam and a fourteen-pointed star for the number of members (including Singapore). The scroll is yellow (the royal colour of Malaysia) on which is inscribed (in two scripts) the Malay motto meaning 'Unity is strength'.

MALDIVE ISLANDS. The State of the Maldives (Al Daulat al Mahldîbîah).
Traditionally these islands, which are a group of atolls in the Indian Ocean to the south-west of Ceylon, were a sultanate; in 1887 they accepted British protection and were placed under Ceylon. They still maintained their sultan and had an elected assembly after 1953 when they were granted internal self-government. The selected form of government then became a republic, but the return to a sultanate came in 1954. On 26 July 1965 the islands were granted independence from Britain and they once more became a republic on 11 November 1968. The State Emblem consists of the Crescent and Star of Islam with two National Flags, in which the red is said to represent the blood sacrificed to gain freedom and the green peace and prosperity. It must be recalled, however, that the islands formerly flew a completely red flag, and that red, white and green are common Moslem colours. Also included are a palm tree—coconuts are exported—and a scroll bearing the name of the State.

BERSEKUTU

BERTAMBAH MUTU

MALI. Republic of Mali (République du Mali).

From the fourth to the nineteenth centuries the region of Mali was the seat of several empires or kingdoms. The medieval empire of Mali, whence the modern republic takes its name, reached its peak in the thirteenth century, but fell in the seventeenth century to Tuareg invaders. The Songhai empire of Gao, which gained control over the settlements along the Niger River, rose to power in the fourteenth century, but was shattered in 1590 by a Moroccan army. In the nineteenth century France began its conquests, and in 1904 it was formed into the colony of French Soudan, which in 1958 voted to join the French Community as an autonomous member with the name of the Sudanese Republic. On 17 January 1959 the Sudanese Republic joined with Senegal to form the Mali Federation, which became independent within the Community on 20 June 1960. The federation was dissolved on 20 August 1960, the components thereafter being independent of each other. The Sudanese Republic withdrew from the Community on 22 September and adopted the name of Mali. The State Emblem displays a dove hovering above a town in the rays of the sun and in the company of two loaded bows; the inscription contains the name of the State and the motto 'One people, one goal, one faith'.

MALTA. The State of Malta.

This island has been under the rule of many States and races in the course of its long and rich history. Phoenicians, Greeks, Romans, Carthaginians, Arabs, Sicilians, French and British have all played their part. Leaving aside early history, from 1530 the island was independent as the home of the Sovereign Military Order of St John. Napoleon took the island away from the Knights of Malta in 1798 and he in turn lost it to the British in 1802; the latter proceeded to annex it in 1814. Although considerable self-government was granted in 1921 the constitution was revoked in 1936 and the island reverted to the status of a crown colony, which so distinguished itself during the Second World War that King George VI awarded the George Cross for bravery to the entire population collectively; that is why the name of the island is sometimes written Malta, G.C. Malta became independent on 21 September 1964 and its State Coat-of-Arms, which was granted by Royal Warrant on 2 September of that year, tells something of its story. Tradition has it that a certain Crusader from Normandy landed on the island in 1094 to drive out the Arabs; the islanders welcomed him and he rewarded them by allowing them to use in their flag the red and white colours of his Arms. However, these are the same colours as the Arms of the Order of Malta and this is the more likely source. To the shield is added a representation of the George Cross. The shield is flanked by two dolphins holding olive and palm branches, reflecting the maritime interests of the island, and is surmounted by the royal helmet bearing as the crest a crown in the form of a castle with a sally-port. The cross of the Knights appears beneath the shield together with the motto meaning 'Through courage and tenacity'.

MAURITANIA (El Mauritanîya; Mauritanie). Islamic Republic of Mauritania (El Djoumhourîyya el Islamîyya El Mauritanîyya; République Islamique de Mauritanie).
The early history of this country is marked by successive invasions of Arabs and Berbers who drove the indigenous Negro tribes to the south; the Berbers in particular made themselves felt, for they destroyed the great Sudanese kingdom of Ghana in the eleventh century and proceeded to conquer North Africa and much of Spain. The descendants of this tribe were known as the Almoravides. The earliest Europeans to arrive were the Portuguese in the fifteenth century; they explored the coasts of Mauretania. In 1815 the French began to penetrate the interior and by 1903 the country had become a French protectorate, being later incorporated into French West Africa. It became a colony in 1920 and in 1946 an overseas territory of France. Becoming an autonomous State within the French Community in 1958 under the present name, it became fully independent on 28 November 1960 and left the Community. The State Seal was adopted at that time and, besides the crescent and star from the National Flag, shows a palm tree and two stalks of millet. The star and crescent (in gold) are sometimes placed upon a green shield to form a State Coat-of-Arms. The inscription on the Seal consists of the name of the State in Arabic and French.

MAURITIUS.
This island in the Indian Ocean was discovered *circa* 1510 by the Portuguese and was occupied at intervals between 1638 and 1712 by the Dutch; settlement was made in 1721 by the French East India Company, which called it Île de France. Although the seat of government was at first on the island of Réunion, it was transferred to Mauritius itself in 1735 and the island became an important base for French operations in India. In the late eighteenth century it was the haunt of privateers who preyed upon British trade with the East and so, in 1814, the British took over the island. The country became fully independent, though recognizing the Queen as Head of State, on 12 March 1968, thus ending 158 years of direct British rule. The State Coat-of-Arms was granted to the crown colony by Royal Warrant on 25 August 1906 and has been retained unchanged; it was based on the old seal of the colony. The ship symbolizes the former immigrants; the key represents the strategic position of the island, while the palm trees stand for the island itself. The star in the fourth quarter, taken in conjunction with the key, illustrates the Latin motto which is rendered 'The Star and Key of the Indian Ocean'. The supporters are a sambur deer and the famous extinct dodo, which was found only in Mauritius; each holds a sugar cane representing the foundation of the island's economy, 90 per cent of the cultivated land being given over to its production.

STELLA CLAVISQUE MARIS INDICI

MEXICO. The United States of Mexico (Estados Unidos Mexicanos).

The first Europeans to visit the coast were Francisco Fernández de Cordoba in 1517 and Juan de Grijalva in 1518; conquest began in 1519 and Cortés defeated the Aztecs in 1521. Such is the brief space of time in which this land was brought under the dominion of Spain, which continued to rule over it for the next three hundred years. Growing discontent with Spanish rule led in due course to open revolt, the beginning of which is marked by the issuing of the *Grito de Dolores* on 16 September 1810; final independence came on 27 September 1821 and the country became an empire under the general Agustín de Iturbide. This, however, was short lived and gave place in 1823 to a republic; in 1864 an empire once more arose under the ill-fated Maximilian, only to be replaced again by a republic in 1867. The State Emblem has seen all these changes and has kept pace with them; it was first adopted in 1823 and the eagle and snake have served ever since as the Emblem or Arms of the successive republics and empires. It will be immediately apparent that the three hundred years of Spanish rule have been judiciously ignored, and in fact the Emblem recalls an old Indian legend; according to this the Aztec people, so it was prophesied, would find their permanent home at the spot where they saw an eagle standing on a cactus and holding a serpent in its beak. This they eventually did, for in A.D. 1325 they built a city on the site of an island in a lake; this is now the centre of Mexico City. The Emblem was re-approved in 1934 and slightly modified in 1968; the plant is a nopal cactus.

MONACO. Principality of Monaco (Principauté de Monaco).

This tiny State, which covers approximately 370 acres, appears to have been settled originally by the Phoenicians and in due course came under Genoese influence. In 1161 the Consuls of Genoa were granted certain rights over this coastal strip, and in 1215 they gave orders for the building of a fortress on the rock overlooking the harbour. At some unknown date the Grimaldi family became Lords of Monaco and firmly established themselves there in 1297; in 1303 it was presented to the Spinola family and in 1338 it was repurchased; in 1356 it was lost again, only to be retaken some time before 1407. The male Grimaldi line has occasionally died out, but the successors have always been relatives by marriage and have assumed the Grimaldi name; this explains the statement which is sometimes heard that the Grimaldi family have been there ever since 1297, although such a statement is manifestly untrue. The Princely Arms are those of the family and are supported by the figures of two Friars Minor brandishing swords; this is a reference to the story that in 1297 Francesco Grimaldi and his men, in the guise of Friars Minor, succeeded in infiltrating the stronghold and overwhelming the garrison. The motto means 'With God's help' and the shield is surrounded by the Collar of the Order of St Charles.

DEO JUVANTE

MONGOLIA (Mongol). Mongolian People's Republic (Bügd Nayramdakh Mongol Ard Uls).
The history of this country is largely the history of the Mongols, and its people are descendants of the warriors who were once led by Genghis Khan. From the seventeenth century until 1911 it was under Chinese control, but the State then set up was invaded by the Chinese in 1919. Outer Mongolia was proclaimed an independent State once again in July 1921 and became a monarchy with Jebtsun Damba Khutukhtu (the Living Buddha of Urga) as sovereign. Upon his death in November 1924 a Communist-led Mongolian People's Republic was established; this is noteworthy because it was the first republic to be so named. The State Emblem was originally adopted in 1940 and was simplified in 1960; it depicts a Mongolian horseman riding into the sun against the background of a typical Mongolian landscape, the whole being surrounded by a wreath of grain which is overlaid by a tricolour ribbon inscribed with the initial letters of the State's title in Cyrillic characters. In the star at the top is the mystic symbol of the Soyonbo which from 1924 to 1940 served as the State Emblem. This has an extremely complex symbolism and may be regarded either as standing for liberty and independence or, as a religious symbol, being akin to the Yin-Yang. The intended significance of the Star and Soyonbo together is the interplay of international proletarian ideals and the national spirit.

MOROCCO (El Maghreb). Kingdom of Morocco (Al Mamlaka al Maghrebîye).
In ancient times Morocco was practically co-extensive with the Roman province of Mauretania Tingitania, and with the collapse of the Roman Empire the land was occupied by the Vandals. The Arabs first swept over the country in 683. European influence followed the expulsion of the Moors from Spain and Portugal. These two countries attacked the Moroccan coast; Portugal took all the main ports except Melilla and Larache, which fell to Spain. Before 1850 France was beginning to advance from the south and all the European powers began to take an interest in the country. On 27 November 1912 the country was divided into three administrative zones—French Morocco, Spanish Morocco and a Southern Protectorate of Morocco. Independence finally came as the result of increasing nationalist agitation on 2 March 1956. The Royal Arms were adopted after independence and exist in two forms; the simpler of these shows the green 'Seal of Solomon' on a red background, while the more complex, here illustrated, also includes a representation of the Atlas mountains with the rising sun. The text on the scroll is taken from the Koran and may be translated 'If you aid God, he will aid you'.

MUSCAT AND OMAN (Musqat wah Oman). Sultanate of Muscat and Oman (Sultanat Masqat wah Oman).

This sultanate was formerly of far greater size than at present and included both Zanzibar and the Baluchistan coast. From 1508 to 1659, when the Turks seized possession, much of the Oman coast was controlled by the Portuguese; the Turks were driven out, however, in 1741 by the founder of the present royal line Ahmed ibn Said of Yemen. In the nineteenth century Oman controlled much of the Persian coast and the coast of Baluchistan; Zanzibar was lost in 1856 and the last foothold in Baluchistan was ceded to Pakistan in 1956, leaving the sultanate with an area of approximately 82,000 square miles of the Arabian peninsula. The State Emblem first made its appearance in 1940 on the coinage, and consists of a native dagger, called a *gambia*, with two crossed scimitars in ornate sheaths.

NAURU. Republic of Nauru.

The small Pacific island of Nauru was discovered by the British in 1798 and was annexed in 1888 by Germany. During the First World War it was occupied by Australian forces and in 1921 was placed under mandate to Australia. It became independent on 1 January 1968 and is affiliated to the British Commonwealth; the world's smallest republic, measuring only eight square miles, it is also one of the richest due to its export of phosphates. There is no State Emblem but merely a National Flag. This was adopted in 1963 and is the result of a competition; blue in colour (for the sky and the Pacific), it bears a yellow horizontal stripe (for the equator) below which is a white twelve-pointed star (for the island itself and its original twelve tribes). The island was formerly called Pleasant Island.

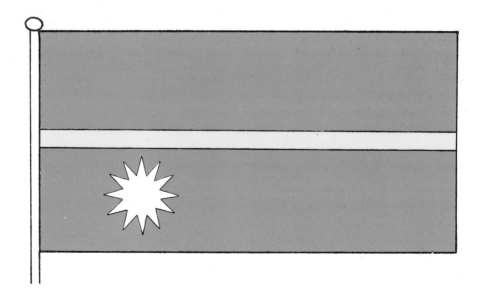

NEPAL. Kingdom of Nepal (Sri Nepalâ Sarkâr).

According to tradition the kingdom of Nepal was founded by the Gupta dynasty of India, but little is known of its history before the fifteenth century. The modern kingdom dates from 1768 when Prithur Narayan Shah, the ruler of Gurkha, incorporated the Valley of Nepal into his kingdom. The country was for some considerable time ruled by a hereditary dynasty of premiers, but in 1951 the King assumed direct control. The present State Emblem shows a Himalayan landscape in which are to be seen a white cow, a pheasant and rhododendron flowers. Above the landscape appear the sun and moon, two crossed Gurkha *kukris*, two Nepalese flags and the footprints of Buddha. The supporters are two Gurkha soldiers, and the Sanskrit motto means 'The Fatherland is worth more than the Kingdom of Heaven'.

THE NETHERLANDS (Nederland). Kingdom of the Netherlands (Koninkrijk der Nederlanden).

Before the sixteenth century the Netherlands had no unified history, but in that century the components passed to the Duke of Burgundy and thence, by marriage, to the House of Habsburg, from which they passed to Spain in 1555. The seven northern provinces declared their independence in 1581 after forming the Union of Utrecht in 1579, and the independence of the United Provinces was finally recognized at the end of the Thirty Years War in 1648. In 1815 the former United Provinces together with the former Austrian Netherlands were given by the Congress of Vienna to the son of William V of Orange, who became King William I of the Netherlands. In 1830 the former Austrian provinces declared their independence and became the Kingdom of Belgium and in 1890 the Grand Duchy of Luxembourg became independent of the Crown. The Royal Arms were adopted in 1815 and are a modification of the hereditary Arms of the House of Nassau, to the lion of which were added a sheaf of arrows and a naked sword. The motto means 'I will maintain'.

JE MAINTIENDRAI

NEW ZEALAND. Dominion of New Zealand.

New Zealand was discovered by the Dutch navigator Abel Janszoon Tasman in 1642 and was visited by Captain James Cook in 1769; in 1814 the first missionary arrived. The islands passed under British sovereignty in 1840 by virtue of the Treaty of Waitangi, under the terms of which the Maoris were guaranteed the full possession of their lands. Self-government was granted by degrees during the nineteenth century, and on 26 September 1907 the Colony of New Zealand became a Dominion with full internal self-government. It became a fully independent member of the British Commonwealth in 1931. The present form of the State Coat-of-Arms dates from 11 July 1957 when Her Majesty approved a revised version of the Arms granted by Royal Warrant on 26 August 1911. The shield contains a representation of the Southern Cross (for the country itself), a fleece and a wheat sheaf (for agriculture), hammers (for the mining industry) and three ships to symbolize the importance of New Zealand's sea trade. The supporters are a European woman (representing the immigrants) and a Maori Rangatira (or chieftain) holding a *taiaha* (or halberd) representing the original inhabitants; they stand upon branches of New Zealand fern, the national plant emblem. The shield is ensigned by the Royal Crown to indicate that Her Majesty is also Queen of New Zealand.

NICARAGUA. Republic of Nicaragua (República de Nicaragua).

This country probably takes its name from Nicarao, an Indian chieftain defeated in 1522 by Gil González de Ávila, who established Spanish rule in the country. After it gained independence from Spain in 1821 it formed part of the Mexican Empire of Iturbide until 1825, when it became part of the Central American Federation. In 1838 it broke away from the Federation and became an independent republic; it was not always free, however, for its east coast was occupied by Britain for twenty years and the United States marines occupied the country from 1912 to 1932. The State Emblem was introduced in 1908 and is very similar to the original emblem of the Central American Union. The equilateral triangle symbolizes equality, truth and justice (although some Nicaraguans say that it also represents the three branches of the government). The five mountains in the sea represent the former members of the United Provinces of Central America, and these are surmounted by a red cap of liberty symbolizing the desire for unity and brotherhood. Over all is the rainbow of hope and sometimes the emblem contains a rising sun on the right.

NEW ZEALAND

NIGER. Republic of Niger (République du Niger).
For a thousand years the region of this country suffered unrest as wave upon wave of invaders poured in, the Semitic and Hamitic peoples ever pressing in upon the domain of the Negroes. The first European to visit the area was Mungo Park in the late eighteenth century; in 1896 the French incorporated the territory into French West Africa and placed it under military rule. In 1921 it became the colony of the Niger. In 1958 it became an autonomous State within the French Community under its present name and achieved complete independence on 3 August 1960. The State Coat-of-Arms was adopted in 1962 and shows a sun accompanied by two crossed Tuareg swords and a lance, and three ears of millet; in base is a buffalo's head. Behind the shield are four National Flags in which the green represents the fertile southern part of the country, the orange the desert, and white stands for purity; the disc in the centre symbolizes the sun.

NIGERIA. The Federal Republic of Nigeria.
Like so many States in Africa this country's history is marked by the rise of many rival States and the growth of regional differences; in the north were the Hausa, in the west the Yoruba and in the south the kingdoms of Ife and Benin. The Portuguese arrived in 1472 and the British followed in 1553; the region soon became an important source of slaves for Europe and the Americas. Gradually palm products replaced slaves as the most important export, and British influence spread rapidly after they had annexed Lagos in 1861 as a base for operations against the slave trade. The British claim to all Nigeria was recognized at the Conference of Berlin in 1885 and the country became a colony in 1914. The Federation became independent on 1 October 1960 and consisted of four autonomous regions, all of which were granted Arms. It became a republic on 1 October 1963. The State Coat-of-Arms was granted by Royal Warrant on 28 April 1960 and represents the country. The shield is black for the name (Niger = black) and bears a white wavy 'pall' to represent the two main rivers, the Niger and the Benue, and their confluence in the heart of the country; black also symbolizes Nigeria's soil. The eagle is symbolic of strength and determination, while the *Coctus spectabilis* flowers, on the compartment upon which the horse supporters stand, are commonly found in Nigeria.

REPUBLIQUE DU NIGER

UNITY AND FAITH

NORWAY (Norge). Kingdom of Norway (Kongeriket Norge).

Before the age of the Vikings the history of Scandinavia as a whole and that of Norway are indistinguishable, since the former was made up of countless petty kingdoms and the latter did not exist as a separate State. In the tenth century A.D. King Harold Fairhair set out on a course of conquest and defeated many petty rulers but he failed to achieve permanent unity. The royal power was not consolidated until the twelfth century and true peace was not enjoyed until the thirteenth century. In 1319 Norway and Sweden were united under one sovereign, and in 1397 they were joined by Denmark; although the union was a purely personal one in the person of the monarch, Norway as an entity virtually ceased to exist and was under the rule of Danish governors for the next four centuries, and its political history became essentially that of Denmark. In 1814 Denmark was obliged to consent to the Treaty of Kiel by which it ceded Norway to the Swedish Crown, which recognized Norway as a separate kingdom with the same sovereign in 1815. Finally in 1905 the union, personal though it was, was dissolved and Norway was once again fully independent; this event took place on 7 June 1905. The Royal Arms were adopted in 1906, but the shield dates from 1280 and the lion is known to occur about A.D. 1200. The battle-axe is that of St Olaf and the Collar of the Order of St Olaf surrounds the shield. The crown and battle-axe commemorate St Olaf, who was King of Norway from 1015 to 1028; he is the patron saint of Norway.

PAKISTAN. Islamic Republic of Pakistan (Jamhuriat-e-Pakistan).

Until this country gained independence on 14 August 1947, its history was largely that of India, with which it shares the great sub-continent. It became a separate entity by virtue of the fact that its population is Moslem by faith, and when it chose to become a republic on 23 March 1956 it did so as the Islamic Republic of Pakistan. The State Coat-of-Arms was adopted in 1955 and the quartered shield displays the four main agricultural products of the country: cotton, tea, wheat and jute. Above the shield appear the Crescent and Star of Islam and the motto, which is given in Urdu and Bengali, means 'Faith, Unity, Discipline'. It will be noted that the entire coat is in green and white, which are favourite colours among Moslems. In 1964 a new symbolic meaning was given to the National Flag and, in view of the close resemblance to this of certain elements in the Arms, it may well be that there has been a similar change in their interpretation. The white is now held to represent peace, while green is for prosperity; the crescent stands for progress, while the star represents light and knowledge. The dual language of the motto is attributable to the division of the country into East and West Pakistan; in the East most people speak Bengali; in the West, although a variety of languages are in everyday use, almost everyone understands Urdu.

PANAMA (Panamá). Republic of Panama (República de Panamá).

Panama was, until 3 November 1903, a part of Colombia and seceded from the latter by means of United States aid. The State Coat-of-Arms was adopted in 1904 and was modified to its present form in 1946; it shows the isthmus at Panama, where it is at its narrowest, and the quarters contain a sabre and rifle (for the war of secession, and hence Panama's history), a hammer and spade (for labour), a cornucopia (for prosperity), and a winged wheel (for progress). The shield is surmounted by an eagle holding a ribbon upon which is the Latin inscription 'For the benefit of the world' in allusion to the Panama Canal. The nine golden stars represent the nine provinces of the country and the country itself is indicated by the crossed National Flags. Originally these were not intended to have any symbolic meaning, but now it is said that the blue section represents the Conservative Party, the red is for the Liberal Party and white stands for peace and unity between these rivals in the cause of independence; the blue star stands for purity and honesty in government and the red one for law and authority.

PARAGUAY. Republic of Paraguay (República del Paraguay).

Paraguay was the first of the South American colonies of Spain to gain independence, and unlike most other countries it achieved freedom and became a republic almost without bloodshed. Its history begins with the exploration of the Rio de la Plata, inspired by the desire to find a new way across the continent; a colony grew up and as time progressed what is now Paraguay gradually attained virtual independence. Indeed real independence was asserted in 1721 when a successful revolt established an independent government which endured for some ten years. A further revolution in 1810 was unsuccessful, but in the following year the colonial officials were quietly overthrown and on 14 May 1811 the Republic of Paraguay was proclaimed. Peace was shattered in 1865 when the combined forces of Brazil, Argentina and Uruguay attacked Paraguay, and the result was disastrous; when the war began the population was some 1,200,000, but at its conclusion in 1870 it had been reduced to a little over 200,000. The State Emblem was officially adopted in 1842, but it may possibly have been in use as early as 1812 when the National Colours—red, white and blue—were chosen. It consists of a golden star, known as the 'Star of May' from the date of independence, enclosed by palm and olive branches tied with a ribbon of the National Colours.

PERU (Perú). Republic of Peru (República del Perú).

The empire of the Incas was a highly developed and highly organized civilization, yet it fell in the course of about a year to Francisco Pizarro, and the country passed under Spanish rule for almost three hundred years. Peru was the last of the South American colonies to gain independence, which was proclaimed by José de San Martin on 28 July 1821. The State Coat-of-Arms was adopted in 1825 after the Spanish forces had finally been overthrown and combines a llama, a cinchona tree and a cornucopia upon the shield to indicate the fauna, flora and minerals of the country. The shield is placed upon four crossed Peruvian flags which recall an incident in the 1820 war. General José de San Martin is said to have seen, as he stepped ashore in Peru, a flock of birds with white breasts and red wings rise up from the shore; choosing to interpret this accident of nature as a happy omen he exclaimed: 'See, the flag of liberty!'

THE PHILIPPINES (Pilipinas). Republic of the Philippines (Republika ñg Pilipinas; República de Filipinas).

The first European to visit these islands was the Portuguese explorer Ferdinand Magellan, who arrived in 1521. Spanish expeditions followed, and to the islands was given the name Las Felipinas, in honour of the Infante Philip (later Philip II), by Lopez de Villalobos in 1542. Conquest did not really begin until 1564, but by 1571 it was virtually complete. The islands erupted in revolution, and independence from Spain was proclaimed 12 June 1898, but in the treaty which ended the war the islands were not given independence but were transferred to the United States of America. True independence had to wait until the end of the Second World War and came peacefully as scheduled on 4 July 1946 when President Truman issued a proclamation recognizing the independence of the Philippines. The State Coat-of-Arms dates from independence and incorporates elements from former coats-of-arms; the lion dates from the Spanish period (1596–1898); the eagle is from the American period (1898–1946); the three stars represent the three main groups of islands; and the sun represents independence, its eight rays indicating the first eight provinces to rise against Spain. The colours combine the Malayan red and white with the American blue; however, red is said to stand for courage, blue for high political ideals and white for purity and peace.

POLAND (Polska). Polish People's Republic (Polska Rzeczpospolita Ludowa).
Little is known about the early history of this country, which became a kingdom in 1025.
In the eighteenth century Poland disappeared from the map as a result of the partitions of
1772, 1793 and 1795, and although the Congress of Vienna (1814–15) had set up a
nominally independent Kingdom of Poland with the Czar of Russia as king, only the
defeat of the partitioning powers in the First World War brought about the country's
independence, which was proclaimed 9 November 1918. By the constitution adopted 22
July 1952 the country became a People's Republic and the State Coat-of-Arms was declared
to be a white eagle on a red shield. This eagle is first found on a seal in 1228 and in 1241
became the Arms of the Kingdom of Poland. These were taken over intact by the new
republic in 1918, but after the Second World War they were brought more into line with
republican trends by omitting the crown which had appeared on the eagle's head; the
characteristic Polish zig-zag border was also omitted.

PORTUGAL. Portuguese Republic (República Portuguesa).
Portugal was born out of the confusion of the reconquest of the Iberian peninsula from
the Moors, and the year 1140, when we find a king styling himself Alfonso I, is generally
taken as the beginning of Portuguese history. By his death in 1185 the country was firmly
established as an independent state, which during the next few centuries began a colonial
expansion of hitherto unrivalled extent. The Madeira Islands and the Azores were colonized,
and by the middle of the sixteenth century the Portuguese king ruled over a vast empire
with territories in South America, Africa, India, China and elsewhere; gradually these
colonies were taken by other powers, and others became independent, until Portuguese
power was left but a shadow of its former self. Portugal itself was ruled by Spain between
1580 and 1640. In 1910 a revolution forced the abdication of King Manoel II, and the
National Assembly of 21 August 1911 sanctioned a republican form of government. The
State Coat-of-Arms adopted by the republic is essentially the Arms of the Royal House of
Braganza, but has been modified to some extent; the shield remains the same, but this is
placed upon an armillary sphere, an old nautical instrument, in reference to Prince Henry
the Navigator and the voyages of discovery which contributed to the country's past
greatness. The border of the shield was added *circa* 1252 after an alliance of the Royal
House with a princess of Castile. Many fanciful legends are related about the origins of the
shields in the Arms, but they are entirely without foundation.

RHODESIA. Republic of Rhodesia.

This country is included in the present work because whatever its *de jure* position might be there can be no doubt that it is *de facto* independent. The country's known history begins in the 1880s when Cecil John Rhodes secured mineral rights from several African chiefs. Lobengula, the Matabele chief, signed a treaty in 1888 making his country a British sphere of influence and in 1890 the British South Africa Company organized the territory and granted land to British settlers. In 1923 Rhodesia was divided into Northern Rhodesia (*see* Zambia) and Southern Rhodesia; the latter became a self-governing colony. In 1953 it became a member of the Federation of Rhodesia and Nyasaland which was dissolved in 1963. In 1965 the country declared its independence, unilaterally, from Great Britain on 11 November and on 2 March 1970 followed up this move by proclaiming itself a republic. The State Coat-of-Arms was granted by Royal Warrant on 11 August 1924 and its principal charge is a pick symbolizing the country's mineral wealth; the lion and thistles are derived from the Arms of Cecil John Rhodes, who gave his name to the country. The crest is a representation of the old African sculpture known as the Great Zimbabwe Bird and the supporters are two sable antelopes. The motto means 'May it be worthy of the name'.

ROMANIA. Rumanian Socialist Republic (Republica Socialistă România).

Romania corresponds roughly to the ancient Dacia, which was a Roman province in the second and third centuries A.D. The country was reduced to vassalage to the Ottoman Empire in the fifteenth century and in the eighteenth century the end of native rule definitely came. At the Congress of Berlin in 1878 the country gained full independence and in 1881 it was proclaimed a kingdom. In December 1947 the king was forced to abdicate and on 30 December a republic was proclaimed; the constitution of 1965 declares it to be a Socialist Republic. The State Emblem was originally adopted in 1948; in 1952 the red star was added and in 1965 the inscription on the ribbon was changed to its present form. As defined in the constitution (Article 109): 'The emblem of the Socialist Republic of Romania represents wooded mountains over which the sun is rising. In the left part of the emblem there is an oil derrick. The emblem is surrounded by a wreath of wheat ears. The emblem is surmounted by a five-pointed star. At the base of the emblem the sheaves are bound with a tricolour ribbon bearing the words "Republica Socialistă România".' The emblem, of course, is a symbolic representation of the country's natural resources.

RWANDA. Republic of Rwanda (Repubulika y'u Rwanda; République Rwandaise).
As with most African countries, the history of Rwanda is a record of successive invasions
by various tribes followed by ultimate annexation on the part of a European power. In
early times the Pygmy Batwa inhabited the plateau regions but were driven out by the
Bahutu who were, in turn in the sixteenth century, conquered by the Watutsi. They
established a kingdom and this continued until very recent times. When Europe began to
carve up Africa, Germany obtained possession of Rwanda in 1886, and when that country
was defeated in 1918 the victorious powers gave it to Belgium, which kept the Tutsi king in
power. The Hutu minority, however, soon became restless and in 1959 came out in open
revolt against both the Tutsi and the Belgians; the Tutsi king, Mwami Kigeri V, went into
exile, and at an election held in September 1961 the people rejected a monarchy and
established a republican regime with a Bahutu-dominated legislature. Belgium agreed to
grant the country its independence and this became official on 1 July 1962. The State
Coat-of-Arms bears a sickle and hoe, representing labour, a bow and arrow, representing
the defence of democratic liberties, and the inscription 'Liberty, Co-operation, Progress'.
Above it is the dove and olive branch of peace and behind it two National Flags in which
red represents the struggle for freedom, yellow the victory of the revolution and green hope.
These are the Pan-African colours, this being further emphasized since the letter R for
Rwanda which appears on the centre of the flag is not visible in the Arms.

EL SALVADOR. Republic of El Salvador (República de El Salvador).
This country was part of the Spanish Empire until 1821 when, in company with Guatemala,
Honduras, Nicaragua and Costa Rica, it declared its independence on 15 September. They
joined together to form the Central American Federation, but this broke up in 1838–9,
leaving the constituent members as individual States. Nevertheless all trace of the
Federation has not entirely vanished, as reference to the Arms of its several members will
indicate. The State Emblem of El Salvador is full of symbolism and is based on the old
Emblem of the Union. The equilateral triangle indicates that all men are equal before the
law; the five volcanoes represent the five former constituent republics of the Union, the
independence of the whole being indicated by the cap of Liberty set upon a pole in the
centre and surrounded by the date of the declaration of independence. The flags set on either
side are also those of the Union. It should be observed that in the motto, which means 'God,
Union and Liberty', the word 'Y' (and) is sometimes omitted.

REPUBLIQUE RWANDAISE

LIBERTE COOPERATION PROGRES

15 de Septiembre de 1821

DIOS UNION LIBERTAD

REPUBLICA DE EL SALVADOR EN LA AMERICA CENTRAL

SAN MARINO. Republic of San Marino (Repúbblica di San Marino).
This small republic, which lies in the hills near Rimini, is entirely surrounded by Italy; yet it has always been independent and its foundation is said to date from the fourth century when a woodcutter from Dalmatia, St Marinus, settled there as a hermit. A settlement grew up around the spot and this has grown into the republic. The people claim that theirs is the oldest republic in the world and the oldest State of all in Europe. It always resisted the papal claims and its integrity was respected by Italy. The State Coat-of-Arms shows three towers crowned with ostrich feathers, each upon a mountain peak; these refer to the fortresses on Monte Titano. The Arms are enclosed within branches of laurel and oak and are surmounted by a crown of sovereignty; the motto means 'Liberty'.

SAUDI ARABIA (Al-'Arabîye as-Sa'udîye). Kingdom of Saudi Arabia (Al Mamlaka al-'Arabîye as-Sa'udîye).
Strictly speaking there is no such country as Saudi Arabia because the kingdom which has been so named since 20 September 1932 is a union of two countries, the Sultan of Nejd being also King of the Hejaz. By the Treaty of Jedda on 20 May 1927 Great Britain recognized Ibn Saud as an independent ruler as King of the Hejaz and Nejd and its dependencies. In the eighteenth century Nejd was an independent State and the stronghold of the Wahhabi sect, which was crushed in 1811 by an Egyptian expedition under Mohammed Ali; a brief revival saw their defeat in 1891 by the Rashid dynasty, which gained effective control of central Arabia. Ibn Saud began the reconquest of the lost lands; he took Riad in 1902 and was master of the Nejd by 1906. The Hejaz fell to him in 1924–5 and was united with the Nejd in 1932 to form the Kingdom of Saudi Arabia. Mohammed was born in Arabia and green is said to have been his favourite colour; for the people of the desert it is the colour of Paradise, and so the State Emblem, which dates from *circa* 1950, is usually shown in this colour. It displays crossed swords (representing Islam's conquests) and a palm tree.

SENEGAL (Sénégal). Republic of Senegal (République du Sénégal).
In the eleventh or twelfth century there was a State of Tekrur along the Senegal River in West Africa; four centuries later the State of Futa took its place, yet this disappeared as the slave traders came upon the scene. To protect these slave traders the Portuguese entered the country and set up forts on the river; the Dutch captured them and later on the French took control. By the end of the nineteenth century Senegal was the centre of French West Africa and in 1946 it became a part of the French Union. The autonomous republic of Senegal was declared on 25 September 1958 and the country elected to remain within the French Community; with the collapse of the Mali Federation in 1960 the republic became completely independent on 20 August. The State Coat-of-Arms was adopted in 1965; the lion represents strength, the baobab tree is indigenous and the green bar represents the Senegal River. From the palm branches which surround the shield hangs the badge of the National Order of the Republic of Senegal; this latter contains the earlier State Coat-of-Arms. The motto means 'One people, one goal, one faith'.

SIERRA LEONE. The State of Sierra Leone.
The name means 'The Mountain Range of the Lion' and this is the name given in 1460 by the Portuguese explorer Pedro da Cintra, because the mountain peaks always seemed to be surrounded by roaring thunderstorms. British interest in the country began with Sir John Hawkins's slave-raiding expedition in 1562, and in the seventeenth and eighteenth centuries it was an important source of slaves. In 1787 Granville Sharp and other abolitionists founded Freetown as a settlement for freed slaves and in 1808 the settlement became a colony. In 1896 the interior became a British protectorate and on 27 April 1961 the whole country became an independent nation within the British Commonwealth. The State Coat-of-Arms was granted by Royal Warrant on 1 December 1960 and contains a pun on the name: the lion and the peaks. The three torches represent freedom and enlightenment, while the wavy bars represent the sea. The palm trees refer to one of the country's most important products—palm oil.

114

UN PEUPLE · UNE FOI · UN BUT

UNITY · FREEDOM · JUSTICE

SINGAPORE. Republic of Singapore.
The word Singhapura, which is the original spelling, means 'City of the Lion' and was given to this seaport by the original indigenous rulers. Until 1819 the island was a part of the State of Johore, but was granted in that year to the British East India Company. It became part of the Straits Settlements in 1826 and on 3 June 1959 became a self-governing State; on 16 September 1963 it became independent as part of the Federation of Malaysia, but withdrew and became a separate republic on 9 August 1965. The State Coat-of-Arms was granted by Royal Warrant on 6 November 1959 and the shield bears the Malayan colours of red and white; the crescent represents the young nation in its ascent towards the ideals represented by the stars: democracy, peace, progress, justice and equality. The lion supporter recalls the significance of the name and the tiger refers to the country's former connection with Malaya; the Malay motto means 'Forward, Singapore!'

SOMALIA (Somaliya). Democratic Republic of Somalia (Al Djumhurîyet as-Somaliye al Demokratîye; _or_ Kharan-ka Somaliya).
This comprises the former British protectorate of British Somaliland and the former Italian trust territory of Somaliland. Most of the former was occupied from the 1870s by Egyptian forces, and the British took their place in 1884; Italian Somaliland was at first a colony, and then a trust territory from 1950 to 1960. Italy first exerted its influence there in 1889 when it established a small protectorate which grew under the Fascist regime; when Italy entered the Second World War it invaded British Somaliland and by August 1940 had occupied the whole territory. The British recovered their territory and took the Italian in 1941, and governed the combined region until 1950 when the trust territory under Italian administration was formed. This was granted internal autonomy in 1956, and independence on 1 July 1960. Britain had already, in June, announced the end of its protectorate and the two States were combined as an act of union of 1 July, thereby producing the Somali Republic; on 25 May 1969 it became a democratic republic. There is strong pressure for the creation of a 'Greater Somalia' which would include all the Somali-speaking peoples, and this is echoed in the State Coat-of-Arms which was adopted in 1954. The colours are taken from the United Nations flag and the star represents African liberty; more specifically its five points refer to the two united provinces and the areas still under foreign rule. By its constitution the area is bound to use peaceful means to unite all five areas. The crown is a symbol of independence and may be due to Italian influence.

MAJULAH SINGAPURA

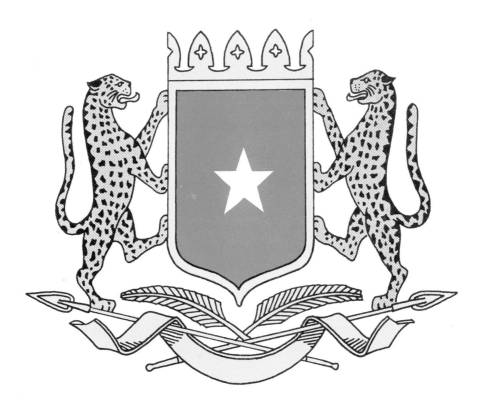

SOUTH AFRICA (Suid Afrika). Republic of South Africa (Republiek van Suid Afrika).
The first European to visit South Africa was the Portuguese Bartholomew Diaz who rounded the Cape of Good Hope in 1488, and the first white settlement was made at Cape Town by the Dutch East India Company in 1652. After several abortive attempts the British took over the colony in 1814, and the Dutch settlers, the Boers, migrated to find new lands for themselves, establishing the republics of Natal, Orange Free State and Transvaal. Great Britain annexed Natal in 1843. The Union of South Africa was inaugurated as a British dominion on 31 May 1910 and on 31 May 1961 became a republic which elected to leave the British Commonwealth. The State Coat-of-Arms, which was granted by Royal Warrant on 17 September 1910, includes symbols alluding to the four provinces; the Cape is represented by a figure of Hope, Natal by two wildebeeste, the Orange Free State by the orange tree and the Transvaal by the trek wagon. The crest of a red lion holding a bundle of rods both illustrates the motto 'Strength from Unity' and originates from the Arms of the old Dutch States General, thus indicating the Dutch origins of the country. The supporters are a springbok and an oryx; the national flower, protea, may be seen in the compartment.

SOUTH YEMEN. People's Republic of South Yemen (Al Djumhurîyet al-Yemenîye al Djanubîye ascha'abîye).
The origin of this republic lies in the British protectorate of Aden which consisted of twenty-four sultanates, emirates and sheikhdoms, and in the colony of Aden itself; the last joined the South Arabian Federation, which was formed in 1959, in 1962. The region was captured by Moslems in 632, and from 1538 until 1609 it was occupied almost continuously by the Turks. Britain stepped in in 1839 and Aden was administered as a part of British India until 1937, when it became a colony. In 1959 the sultanates of Andhali, Fadhli and Lower Yafa, the emirates of Beiban and Dhala and the sheikhdom of Anlaqi, founded the Aden Federation despite the strong protests of the Yemen, which claimed the protectorate. In 1962 Aden joined the Federation, which then became the South Arabian Federation. On 30 November 1967 it became independent as the People's Republic of South (or Southern) Yemen. The State Coat-of-Arms has been based on Egyptian and Yemeni emblems and shows the 'Saladin' eagle with a breast-shield of the National Flag; the three stripes formed the flag of the ruling party, the National Liberation Front, before independence which is represented by the star; the red represents revolution, white peace and black the extermination of colonialism. The triangle represents the people.

118

EX UNITATE VIRES

جمهورية اليمن الجنوبية الشعبية

SPAIN (España). The Spanish State (Estados Español).

Spain is a monarchy temporarily without a monarch since the abdication of Alfonso XIII in 1931; his grandson, Prince Juan Carlos de Borbon y Borbon, was sworn heir to the throne in 1969 and given the title of Prince of Spain. Although Spain had made such a mark on the world at large by its colonial expansion there was no such State until 1492 when the fall of Granada made Isabella I and Ferdinand V rulers of the whole land; hitherto the country had been brought together bit by bit. Navarre originally controlled Aragon and Castile, but on the death of Sancho III his kingdom split into its three parts: Aragon united with Barcelona in 1137 and Castile united with Leon in 1230 and joined Aragon in 1479. This explains the somewhat crowded shield which serves as the State Coat-of-Arms, and was introduced in its present form in 1938; the quarters represent Castile (a castle), Leon (a lion), Aragon (red stripes on yellow), Navarre (the chains) and Granada (the pomegranate). These quarterings go back to about 1500. The old Roman symbol of state, the eagle, is flanked by the Pillars of Hercules ensigned by the imperial and royal crowns. These have the inscription 'Plus ultra' to indicate that the country extended beyond the Straits of Gibraltar after the discovery of America. The yoke and arrows are old Spanish symbols and were the badges of Isabel and Ferdinand. The motto means 'One great free (realm)'.

SUDAN. Democratic Republic of the Sudan (Al Djumhurîyet as-Sudan al demokratîye).

Under no circumstances must this State be confused with the former Sudanese Republic; this is now the Republic of Mali and lies on the other side of Africa. Sudan, or rather 'Bilad-as-Sudan', meaning 'Land of the Black People', is the name given to the whole continent by the Arabs who, when they began to move southwards, were surprised to find that the Nubians were not alone in having dark skins. From 1822 onwards the Egyptians gradually conquered the Nile Valley, thus reversing a process which had taken place some thousands of years before, and governed it until the 1880s when it was overrun by the Mahdi. From 1899 to 1956 the country was an Anglo-Egyptian condominium, and the country became independent on 1 January 1956; on 25 May 1969 it adopted its present title. The State Emblem, adopted in 1970, is a stylized representation of the bearded vulture (*lammergeier*), which has a scroll above its head bearing the Arabic motto 'Victory for Us'. The scroll below bears the name of the State. The former State Emblem is illustrated here, however, since official copies of the present one were not available.

جمهورية السودان

SWAZILAND. Kingdom of Swaziland.

This country was occupied in 1820 by the Swazi tribe, who had been driven from their original home north of the Pongola River by another tribe. By the inhabitants it is called *Ka Ngwame*, and before this book appears in print it is quite likely that this will be its official name. Europeans first settled there in the 1880s, and in 1888 the Swazi king allowed them self-government. In 1894 the country became a British protectorate and as a high commission territory was ruled by a British commissioner; it received independence on 6 September 1968. The State Coat-of-Arms, which was adopted in 1968, bears the ox-hide shield of an Emahsotsha warrior whose feathered head-dress forms the crest. The blue ornamental tassels on the staff which accompanies the spears are royal attributes. The motto, which means 'We are the strength', refers to the lion and elephant supporters.

SWEDEN (Sverige). Kingdom of Sweden (Konungariket Sverige).

Sweden has been a kingdom since *circa* A.D. 800 and its modern declared neutrality contrasts strangely with its history, for it has seen rather more than its fair share of wars. In the early historic period the land was inherited by the Svears, whence the name, and by the sixth century they succeeded in conquering their southern neighbours the Gotar, with whom they merged. In 1319 Sweden and Norway were united under Magnus VII and in 1397 the crowns of Sweden, Norway and Denmark were united in the person of Queen Margaret in what is known as the Kalmar Union. Her successors were unable to control the Swedes and in 1523 the country broke away; in 1814 the Congress of Vienna awarded Norway to Sweden and this union lasted until 1905. The State Arms are more fully described in terms of their historical evolution in the Introduction, but we must note that the Great Coat-of-Arms was last approved by the Act of 15 May 1908. The quarters of the shield *all* represent Sweden, although the lion coat is sometimes said to belong to Gotaland; the narrow cross separating them is derived from the National Flag and may have been inspired by the Dannebrog of Denmark. The smaller shield bears the Arms of the Royal House (Vasa impaling Bernadotte). The whole coat is surrounded by the Collar of the Order of the Seraphim.

SIYINQABA

MEDFOLKET FOR FOSTERLANDET

SWITZERLAND (Schweiz; Suisse; Svizzera; Svizera). The Swiss Confederation (Schweizerische Eidgenossenschaft; Confédération Helvétique; Confederazione Helvetica; Cónfederaziun Svizera).

Switzerland has no fewer than four official languages; German, French, Italian and . Romansh; this explains the large number of terms which have been used to give the titles above. It also explains something of the country's complexity; it is a union of many mountain-valley communities which came together in defence of their freedom. There are in fact twenty-five federated states consisting of nineteen cantons and six half-cantons, together forming twenty-two cantons. The country fell in 58 B.C. to the Romans and thereafter it passed through a succession of hands until it became divided between the Houses of Habsburg and Savoy; the coming together of the various states led to the formation of the State, and its independence was formally recognized by the Peace of Westphalia in 1648. The Swiss Confederation was formed on 1 August 1291 and the following are the cantons (each of which has its own Arms) with the dates on which they were adopted into the Confederation; the official Swiss sequence is adopted. Zürich (1351), Berne (1353), Lucerne (1332), Uri (1291), Schwyz (1291), Obwalden, or Unterwalden ob dem Wald (1291), Nidwalden, or Unterwalden nid dem Walden (1291), Glarus (1352), Zug (1352), Fribourg (1481), Solothurn (1481), Basel-Stadt (1501), Basel-Land (1501, 1832), Schaffhausen (1501), Appenzell-Innerhoden (1513), Appenzell-Ausserhoden (1513), St Gallen (1803), Graubünden (1803), Aargau (1803), Thurgau (1803), Ticino (1803), Vaud (1803), Valais (1815), Neuchâtel (1815) and Geneva (1815). The State Coat-of-Arms, which was formally decreed in 1814 and reaffirmed in 1941, is known from the fourteenth century and is a symbol of the struggle for freedom.

SYRIA (As Suriya). The Syrian Arab Republic (Al Djumhurîet al-'Arabîye as Surîye).

In the distant past this country has formed a part of the great empires, the Hittite, Egyptian, Babylonian, Persian, Macedonian, Seleucid and Roman; in the seventh century A.D. it became the centre of the Arab Empire with Damascus as the capital. Later on the country was ruled by various foreign invaders, including the Crusaders and the Mongols, but in 1512 the Ottoman Empire established control and under that sway it remained, almost without remission, until the end of the First World War. France then took control and ruled until 1 January 1944, when Syria became independent. From 1 February 1958 to 30 September 1961 it formed with Egypt the United Arab Republic. The State Coat-of-Arms, which dates from independence, although the breast-shield was changed to its present form in 1963, is notable as being the first in the Arab world to be based on a heraldically stylized eagle. However, although this has inspired all the other Arab eagles, it differs from them: it is not the 'Saladin' eagle, which is even more stylized. The scroll bears the name of the republic in Arabic and the two ears of corn refer to the country's most important industry, agriculture.

TANZANIA. United Republic of Tanzania (Djumhurîyet Tanzania).
Apparently Tanganyika, which forms part of the United Republic, must have been one of the earliest homes of mankind; the very earliest fossilized bones have been found there and Man may have begun there some two million years ago. If this is so, then this country's history must be longer than that of any other land, but it is only known from the eighth century when the Arabs began to settle. It was ruled from Zanzibar, but the area was inhabited by more or less independent tribes; as with so many other countries, the first European contact was made by the Portuguese, who began exploration *circa* 1500. They held it loosely until the seventeenth century when they were supplanted by the Arab sultans of Muscat who were, in turn, replaced by the Germans who founded the colony of German East Africa in 1884. The country became a British mandate under the League of Nations in 1920, and in 1945 was made a United Nations trust territory. Independence was achieved on 9 December 1961, and Tanganyika united with Zanzibar on 26 April 1964 to form Tanzania. The State Coat-of-Arms dates from the union, but is a modification of the one granted by Royal Warrant on 6 September 1961. The torch represents liberty and enlightenment and in the division below it appears the National Flag. The compartment is a representation of Mount Kilimanjaro with a coffee plant and a cotton plant, the supporters being a man and woman. The motto means 'Liberty and Unity'. The arms are significant in that they were the first (1961) to be shown upon an African warrior's shield.

THAILAND (Thai). Kingdom of Thailand (Prades Thai, *or* Muang Thai).
The Thai people came from China, where their kingdom of Nanchao was overrun by the Mongols in 1253; migration to Thailand had begun in A.D. 650 but when they finally moved out they set up a kingdom which was never to become a colony of any European power; indeed, European bids for power served only to strengthen the country's autonomy. The Thai name for their country is 'Land of the Free'. The national faith is Buddhism and this is reflected in the Royal Emblem which was adopted in 1910 by King Rama VI (P'ra Paramin Maha Vajiravudh). When borne upon the Royal Standard it is in red on golden yellow. It depicts the Kroot or Garuda Bird, the Chief of the Feathered Race; apart from being immortal, this mythological bird served as the mount of Phra Narai, who in reincarnation became Phra Ram, the heroic king and conqueror in the legend 'Rammakien'. He is the enemy of the serpent race and is represented as having the head, wings, talons and beak of an eagle; blessed with superhuman qualities, the Kroot took on the features of a man. He is the younger brother of Phra Arun (The Dawn) who served as charioteer to Phra Artit (The Sun). In terms which may be more easily understood in the West it may be said that this bird is the mightiest of all and served as the mount of the god Vishnu.

TOGO. The Togolese Republic (République Togolaise).

European penetration of Togoland started in 1840 when German missionaries began to arrive, and in 1884 Germany declared a protectorate over the region. During the First World War the region was occupied by British and French troops; in 1922 the League of Nations divided the territory into French and British mandates which became in 1946 trust territories of the United Nations. The British mandated territory gained independence in 1957 as part of the State of Ghana; the French mandated territory gained independence as the Republic of Togo on 27 April 1960. The State Coat-of-Arms was adopted in 1962 and includes a shield bearing the initials of the State; this is guarded, rather than supported (since their backs are towards the shield), by two lions symbolizing the courage of the Togolese; and holding a bow and arrow. Their attitude officially indicates the alertness of the people. The motto means 'Work, Freedom, Fatherland', and above the shield appear two National Flags. In these there are two explanations of the symbolism; the first would have the green to represent hope and agriculture, the yellow for the peasants' faith in the importance of their work, the red for charity, faithfulness, love and sacrifice for humanity; white for purity. The other explanation gives yellow for mineral resources, red for the blood shed in the struggle for independence and the white star for hope and wisdom.

TONGA. Kingdom of Tonga.

The Kingdom of Tonga comprises some two hundred islands in the South Pacific occupying an area of 250 square miles; the northern ones were discovered in 1616 by the Dutch and the rest of the group by Tasman in 1643. Captain James Cook visited them in 1773 and called them the Friendly Islands, a name which belied his reception. English missionaries began to arrive in 1797 and their presence helped to strengthen British political influence. The islands were first united in 1845 by King George Tubou I and the kingdom accepted British protection on 18 May 1900; complete independence, in affiliation with the British Commonwealth, was attained on 4 June 1970. The State Coat-of-Arms was designed in 1862 by a Tongan prince and represents a Christian kingdom; the three stars represent the three main groups of islands, Tongatabu, Vavau and Haabai; the dove represents the spirit of Christianity; the crown represents the monarchy and the three swords represent the three royal dynasties. The six-pointed star with the red cross is the device of the nation; this cross is interesting because not only does it indicate that the islands are Christian, being coloured red to symbolize the blood shed by Our Lord upon the Cross, but by virtue of its being a Greek cross is of the same pattern as that used in the badge of the Methodist Conference, to which denomination the islanders adhere. Two pennants bearing this cross appear from behind the shield.

TRINIDAD AND TOBAGO. The Territory of Trinidad and Tobago.
As Columbus's ships approached the islands in 1498 the crews saw before them three prominent peaks (the Three Sisters) and these prompted him when he landed on 1 August at Punta de la Playa (Erin Point) on the larger of the two islands to give it the name of Trinidad (Trinity). There he hoisted the royal standard of Ferdinand and Isabella and claimed the land for Spain. The lack of precious metals, however, meant that few Spanish settlers were attracted and there was no permanent settlement until 1592. In the succeeding centuries the Dutch, French and British all laid claim to the islands; the British eventually won, Tobago being ceded in 1763 and Trinidad becoming British in 1797. The islands became independent on 31 August 1962. The State Coat-of-Arms was granted by Royal Warrant on 9 August 1962 and incorporates the national colours; black stands for the islanders' devotion to national unity; red for the vitality of the people and their land; and white for the sea, the purity of the people's aspirations and the equality of all men under the sun. The three ships represent the Trinity and also the fleet of Columbus; the humming-birds (*Phaethornis guy guy*) were included for 'sentimental' reasons; the ship's wheel refers to the importance of shipping to the islands and the fruited coconut palm is derived from the Great Seals of British Colonial Tobago. The supporters are a scarlet ibis (*Eudocimus ruber*) for Trinidad and a cocrico (*Ortalis ruficauda ruficauda*) for Tobago; these stand on a compartment representing the two islands set in the sea.

TUNISIA (Al Tunis). Tunisian Republic (Al Djumhurîyet al-Tunisîye).
The region of Tunisia was settled by the Phoenicians nearly three thousand years ago and in the sixth century B.C. it passed to Carthage, later becoming one of the granaries of Rome. Afterwards it fell to the Vandals and the Byzantine Empire, but in the seventh century it was conquered by the Arabs; in the late sixteenth century it became a Turkish domain which in 1881 became a French protectorate. This gained independence on 20 March 1956 and in 1957 the monarchy was overthrown. The present State Coat-of-Arms was introduced in 1963 and is based on a design which during the monarchy had replaced the traditional Arms of Tunisia. It may be said to illustrate the motto, which means 'Order, Freedom, Justice'.

TOGETHER WE ASPIRE   TOGETHER WE ACHIEVE

TURKEY (Türkiye). Republic of Turkey (Türkiye Cümhuriyeti).

The history of this country is so long and rich as to be impossible to summarize. Its peak of power, however, came with the Ottoman Empire, whose beginnings can be traced back to 1296, when the Osmanli Turks were granted lands on the frontier with the Byzantine Empire by their overlords, the Seljuk Turks. The Ottoman Empire was dealt its death-blow in the First World War and the Treaty of Sèvres, in 1920, reduced one of the great universal states of modern times to a small State comprising the northern half of the Anatolian peninsula and a narrow, neutralized and Allied-occupied zone on the Straits. On 1 November 1922 the Ankara Government declared the sultan to be deposed and on 29 October 1923 Turkey became a republic. The State Emblem is the crescent and star of Islam, which had been that of the old Ottoman Empire. The origin of these symbols is obscure, but it is certain that the Turks did not invent them; whatever they may have represented originally, they have come to be the most popular Moslem emblem throughout the world. In 1927 the republic devised new Arms to replace those of the sultanate, but these are now seldom, if ever, seen; the star and crescent were retained and set above the white wolf of the Turks standing on a lance, thus recalling the totem symbol of the tribal state of nomads in central Asia which was to become the Turkish people.

UGANDA. Republic of Uganda.

British explorers were among the first to reach the country, and in 1877 Anglican missionaries arrived; in 1888 Arab traders and native Moslems destroyed the mission settlements and this led, in 1894, to the proclamation of a protectorate over the holdings of the British East Africa Company which had been granted in 1890. In the period 1896 to 1914 several other neighbouring states and tribal lands were annexed and the whole country was firmly under British rule. It gained independence on 9 October 1962 and on the same date in 1963 became a republic. The State Coat-of-Arms was granted on 3 September 1962 and is depicted on an African warrior's shield. The drum symbolizes the kingdoms and culture of Uganda and the sun refers to the fact that the country lies astride the Equator; the waves refer to the great lakes and the sources of the Nile. Behind the shield are two crossed spears of state, and the shield is supported by a kob and a crested crane, both being indigenous to the country and the latter having served as the colonial badge for Uganda, on a compartment showing a conventional representation of a divided river and a coffee and a cotton plant.

FOR GOD AND MY COUNTRY

THE UNION OF SOVIET SOCIALIST REPUBLICS (Soyuz Sovietskikh Sotsialisticheskikh Respublik) (U.S.S.R.).

Historical summary must be superfluous; the State Emblem of the Union tells sufficient of the story itself. As defined in the constitution of the U.S.S.R. (Chapter XII, Article 143): 'The arms of the Union of Soviet Socialist Republics are a sickle and a hammer against a globe depicted in the rays of the sun and surrounded by ears of grain, with the inscription "Workers of All Countries, Unite!" in the languages of the Union Republics. At the top of the arms is a five-pointed star.' This State Emblem has provided the model for those subsequently adopted for most Communist States and it repays further study. The idea behind the emblem, which was adopted in 1922, is the emergence of the new golden era and the spread of Communist ideals across the world; the hammer represents the workers and the sickle represents the peasants, the wreath of grain being indicative of agriculture. The languages in which the inscription appears are, reading from top to bottom, those of (on the left) the Turkmen SSR, Tajik SSR, Latvian SSR, Lithuanian SSR, Georgian SSR, Uzbek SSR, Ukrainian SSR, (on the right) Estonian SSR, Armenian SSR, Kirghiz SSR, Moldavian SSR, Azerbaijanian SSR, Kazakh SSR, Byelorussian SSR and (at the base) the Russian SFSR. The five-pointed star represents the unity of the working people of the five continents, Europe and Asia being counted as one.

UNITED KINGDOM. The United Kingdom of Great Britain and Northern Ireland.

The unification of Great Britain has been a protracted affair and the actuality has always preceded the formality; England itself became subject to a single monarch only in A.D. 829, but even then it was a precarious situation. The conquest of Ireland began in the reign of Henry II, that of Wales in the reign of Edward I, who also tried to subdue Scotland. Union between Wales and England was achieved in 1536; Scotland came under the same sovereign as England (or rather *vice versa*) in 1603, but union did not occur until 6 March 1707; union with Ireland took place on 1 January 1801. A more detailed account than is here possible of the development of the Royal Arms is given in our introduction. but it may be pointed out that of the Arms appearing as quarterings on the shield, those of England are first found on the second Great Seal of Richard I, those of Scotland on that of Alexander III (1249–86) and those of Ireland appear to date from Henry VIII's elevation of the lordship into a kingdom. The version we illustrate is the English one, the version appearing on Her Majesty's Great Seal for Scotland being somewhat different. Arms, etc., also exist for the kingdom of Scotland and for the Government of Northern Ireland.

THE UNITED STATES OF AMERICA (U.S.A.).

It is surely not necessary to give any explanation of the historic events which led to the foundation of the first republic in the Western Hemisphere. What may not be so readily understood and what is sometimes most strongly denied is that there is no State Coat-of-Arms for the republic. Nevertheless this is a fact; what the Continental Congress approved on 20 June 1782 was the design for the Great Seal of the republic and the inclusion of Armorial Bearings in the design is purely incidental. The reverse is every bit as important as the obverse, but has tended to be overshadowed by the latter. On the obverse the American eagle holds a shield derived from the first flag in which the thirteen stripes represent the thirteen original states bound together in a unity; the stars above the head also have the same significance. The eagle holds in its talons the olive branch of peace and the arrows of war—significantly thirteen in number. The motto means 'Out of many, one'. The reverse bears the date of the founding of the nation, 1776; an unfinished pyramid to suggest the firm and durable building of the new nation which nevertheless had room for other states; a single eye surrounded by the sun's rays to suggest the eye of Providence surrounded by the light of the universe. There are also two inscriptions; the first (*Annuit Coeptis*) means 'He has favoured our undertaking' and the second (*Novus Ordu Seclorum*) means 'A new order of the ages', both being adapted from the Latin poet Virgil.

UPPER VOLTA (Haute-Volta). Republic of Upper Volta (République de Haute-Volta).

In pre-colonial times the region was dominated by the Moro Naba Empire of the Mossi whose origins are lost in obscurity; they conquered territory as far north as Timbuktu. Their empire disintegrated and part of their land became, for a time, part of the Moslem Empire of Mali; much later, in 1896, the French established a protectorate which in 1919 was converted into the colony of Upper Volta. In 1932 the country was divided, for administrative convenience, between the Ivory Coast, French Sudan and Niger, but in 1947 was reconstituted as a separate territory which attained full independence on 5 August 1960, having gained self-governing status within the French Union on 11 December 1958. The State Coat-of-Arms dates in its present form from 1967; this differs from the original version adopted in 1961 by the presence of an African shield in place of a European one and the omission of the letters R.H.V. The shield is divided in the national colours which recall that the three main branches of the river are called the Black, the White and the Red Volta; behind it are placed a spear and a sorghum (millet) plant. Issuing from the motto scroll which reads in translation 'Unity, Work, Justice' are two hoes; the supporters are two white horses which appear to have no particular significance.

UNITE TRAVAIL JUSTICE

URUGUAY. The Eastern Republic of Uruguay (República Oriental del Uruguay).

The Spanish began to explore the Rio de la Plata in 1515, but it was not until 1624 that they established their first settlement in Uruguay; the Portuguese in competition established a settlement at Montevideo in 1717, but were driven out by the Spanish in 1724. When the revolutionary campaigns began in Argentina in 1810 the leaders of the Banda Oriental took up the cause, but eventually they directed their efforts towards securing their own independence. This was frustrated in 1820 by the Brazilian occupation of Montevideo, but on 25 August 1825 a small group known as the Thirty-three Immortals declared the country independent, and in 1827 Brazil was defeated. The State Emblem was originally adopted in 1829 and the present design dates from 1908; the oval cartouche includes the golden scales of justice, the 'cerro' of Montevideo with a fortress on its summit as a symbol of power, a wild horse for freedom and liberty, and a gold bull for the source of Uruguay's wealth—cattle-breeding. The wreath of olive and laurel was added in 1906 and the 'Sun of May' is a reminder of the country's former affiliation with Argentina; in this context, of course, it represents the independence of Uruguay.

THE VATICAN CITY (Città del Vaticano). State of the Vatican City (Stato della Città del Vaticano).

This independent, sovereign State of 108 acres lies in the very heart of Italy and may, perhaps, be looked upon as part of Rome itself. Nevertheless it must be conceded that parts of the city of Rome and its surroundings are not in Italy but belong to the Vatican State. This curious state of affairs arises from the fact that the Vatican City is the remains of the Papal States which were founded in A.D. 715. They disappeared with the unification of Italy, but the Vatican remained resolutely independent and was once more recognized by Italy as a sovereign State by the Lateran Treaty, which was signed on 11 February 1929. The Arms of the State are those of the Holy See, since His Holiness the Pope is its sovereign and has as his official title 'Bishop of Rome, Vicar of Jesus Christ, Successor of the Prince of the Apostles, Supreme Pontiff of the Universal Church, Patriarch of the West, Primate of Italy, Archbishop and Metropolitan of the Roman Province, Sovereign of the State of the Vatican City'.

VENEZUELA. Republic of Venezuela (República de Venezuela).
In 1498 Christopher Columbus discovered the mouth of the Orinoco River; in 1499 the coast was explored by Alonso de Ojeda and Amerigo Vespucci and the latter, coming upon an island which had Indian villages built upon piles over the water, nicknamed it Venezuela, 'Little Venice'; the name persisted and became attached to the mainland. On 5 July 1811 independence from Spain was declared, this being sealed by the victory at Carabobo in 1821. Venezuela and other territories then became part of the federal republic of Gran Colombia, but in 1830 it separated and became an independent State. The State Coat-of-Arms was introduced in 1836 and was most recently redefined in 1963; upon it an untamed white horse roams the *llanos* (broad plains) under the blue skies. This represents both liberty and the expansive tracts of open country. Above this are a golden wheatsheaf to represent both agricultural wealth and unity, and a trophy of tricolour flags and weapons to represent military triumph; the flags are those of Gran Colombia. Above the shield are placed two cornucopias representing wealth, and the shield is placed within a wreath of laurel and palm. The inscription on the ribbon, which is in the national colours, was changed to its present form on 15 April 1953, and in addition to the name of the State gives the date of the beginning of the revolution (19 April 1810) and of federation (10 February 1859).

VIET NAM. Democratic Republic of Viet Nam (Viet-Nam Dân Chù Công Hoà).
Viet Nam became independent in A.D. 939 when the Viets, who had been driven out of central China some centuries before, drove off their masters the Chinese; with intervals it remained independent until 1859, when the French captured Saigon. Shortly afterwards the colony of Cochin China was organized. In 1884 France declared protectorates over Tonkin and Annam and by the end of the century French Indo-China included Cochin China, Annam, Tonkin and Laos. During the Second World War the country was occupied by the Japanese and when the French tried to bring about the return of French rule they met with resistance. The Viet Minh Party declared their independence and set up a republic with its capital at Hanoi on 11 March and 29 August 1945 respectively. The State Emblem was adopted in 1956 and consists of a five-pointed star, representing the five sections of the population (peasants, workers, intellectuals, young people and soldiers), on a red field (for revolution) which is set within a garland of ears of rice (for agriculture) at the base of which is a cogwheel (for industry). The scroll is inscribed with the name of the State.

140

VIET NAM. Republic of Viet Nam (Viet-Nam Công Hoà).

A few months after the armistice of 1954, which partitioned the country at the 17th parallel of latitude, South Viet Nam withdrew from the French Union and so attained complete sovereign independence; on 26 October 1955 it was proclaimed a republic. The State Coat-of-Arms was adopted in 1963 to bring it into accordance with the National Flag, though in the Arms the red lines are upright. The yellow background is the traditional colour of the fatherland and also symbolizes the golden rice; the three red bars represent North, Central and South Vietnam as one nation and recall the country's name: Viet Nam means 'the Southern Land' and three parallel lines are the Chinese ideogram for the word 'South'. The State Coat-of-Arms is sometimes seen with dragon supporters; these are the oriental symbols of power and magnanimity.

WESTERN SAMOA (Samoa i Sisifo).

The first recorded visit of Europeans to the islands of Samoa took place in 1722 and the people involved were Dutch; in 1830 a Christian missionary from Britain came to stay and subsequently Britain, the United States and Germany began to trade in the islands. A tripartite treaty in 1889 proclaimed the islands to be neutral territory, but in 1899 Britain and Germany assigned to the United States all the islands lying to the east of 170°; the islands to the west of this line were assigned to Germany. In 1920 these latter were mandated to New Zealand by the League of Nations and in 1946 they became a United Nations trust territory under New Zealand control. The territory became independent on 1 January 1962 and is affiliated to the British Commonwealth. The State Coat-of-Arms dates from independence and has as its principal charge a representation of the Southern Cross; this is derived from the National Flag, the ultimate source being the flag of New Zealand. The palm tree is taken from the flag badge of the former trust territory and the cross stands for the Christian faith professed by the people.

FA AVAE I LE ATUA SAMOA

THE YEMEN (Al Yemen). The Yemeni Arab Republic (Al Djumhurîyet al-'Arabiye al-Yemenîye).

The Arabic name of the country probably means 'the right hand' and so describes its position relative to a person standing before the Kaaba in Mecca and facing east. At an early period it enjoyed a high degree of civilization, and that which flourished from *circa* 750 B.C. to *circa* 115 B.C. was technically advanced; about 650 B.C. an irrigation dam was built in the mountains at Marib and remained in use until A.D. 572 when it broke and was never repaired. After passing by way of conquest through several hands, the country fell to the Ottoman Empire in 1520 and remained under that rule until the end of the First World War. From the mid nineteenth century the country was ruled, under the Turks, by an *imam* (a Moslem leader with absolute power) who was overthrown in a revolution, a republic being declared on 26 September 1962. In October 1970 it was announced that the republic had overcome the remaining royalist forces; Saudi Arabia has recognized the republic and there is once again a single regime. The State Emblem was adopted after 1965 to replace the one adopted after the setting up of the republic; this was exactly similar to the State Emblem of the United Republic but the stars on the breast-shield numbered only one. The new emblem retains the 'Saladin' eagle, which now faces the other way, and upon its breast are placed a torch and two crossed National Flags which are surmounted by a triangle depicting the old Marib dam with a branch of the coffee tree above it. The scroll, as is usual, bears the name of the State.

YUGOSLAVIA (Jugoslavija). Socialist Federal Republic of Yugoslavia (Socijalistička Federativna Republika Jugoslavija).

Yugoslavia first came into existence as a result of the First World War, and its earlier history is more correctly the history of its component lands. In 1914 only Serbia and Montenegro were independent States; Croatia, Slovenia, Bosnia and Herzegovina were under the Austro-Hungarian monarchy. On 4 December 1918 the South Slavic peoples proclaimed 'The Kingdom of the Serbs, Croats, and Slovenes' and this remained its somewhat cumbersome title until 1929, when it was renamed Yugoslavia. On 29 November 1945 the Constituent Assembly proclaimed the country a republic and in 1946 it became a federal republic. The new constitution of 1963 proclaimed it as a 'Socialist republic'. The State Emblem dates from 1946, but contained only five torches until 1963, when the number was increased to the present six. These represent the six constituent republics, each of which has its own State Emblem. The wreath of ears of wheat is combined with the usual five-pointed red star and is entwined with a ribbon, which may be in any one of the national colours (red, white, blue) inscribed with the official date of the founding of the Yugoslav Federal Republic.

ZAMBIA. Republic of Zambia.

The early history of the former Northern Rhodesia is largely unknown, but it would appear that the country was subject to frequent invasions from the surrounding lands; in the seventeenth and eighteenth centuries, in particular, it was harassed by the activities of Arab and Portuguese slave traders. Missionaries from Scotland settled on the banks of the Zambesi River in the 1840s and David Livingstone passed through in 1851; next came traders, gold miners and, finally, British administration. Barotseland (the south-west) was made a British protectorate in 1891 and by 1894 the British had gained control of the eastern portion also. The boundaries of Northern Rhodesia were established in 1911 and Great Britian took over direct rule in 1924. From 1953 to 1963 it was a part of the Federation of Rhodesia and Nyasaland, and on 24 October 1964 it became an independent republic within the Commonwealth. The State Coat-of-Arms adopted in 1965 is based upon the Arms granted by Royal Warrant on 16 August 1939 to the former colony of Northern Rhodesia; the eagle which appeared on the original shield has now lost its fish and is placed above a crossed hoe and pick above and outside the shield. This osprey is the symbol of Zambia's freedom and aspirations. The shield itself represents the Victoria Falls which were discovered by Livingstone in 1855; the compartment, upon which stand a Zambian man and woman supporting the shield, includes a mining installation, a maize cob and a zebra.

QATAR. The Emirate of Qatar.

This Arab State, which attained complete independence on 1 September 1971, occupies and is co-terminous with the Qatar peninsula, which projects into the Persian Gulf. Although it never truly lost its independence, it was, like the neighbouring Trucial States, under British protection from the first half of the nineteenth century. The treaty arrangements were designed to prevent piracy and slavery and to maintain a perpetual truce in regard to all hostile acts at sea. The economy depends upon fishing, including pearl fishing, and particularly the oil industry. Qatar became a part of the Federation of Arab Emirates of the Persian Gulf on 30 March 1968 and its State Emblem dates from 1966. It consists of two scimitars, a pearl oyster shell and the name of the country, surrounded by two palm branches.

ONE ZAMBIA ONE NATION